What Really Matters?

What Really Matters?

Ten Critical Issues in Contemporary Education

Bernard Bull

WIPF & STOCK · Eugene, Oregon

WHAT REALLY MATTERS?
Ten Critical Issues in Contemporary Education

Wipf & Stock
An Imprint of Wipf and Stock Publishers
199 W. 8th Ave., Suite 3
Eugene, OR 97401

www.wipfandstock.com

PAPERBACK ISBN: 978-1-4982-9240-5
HARDCOVER ISBN: 978-1-4982-9242-9
EBOOK ISBN: 978-1-4982-9241-2

Manufactured in the U.S.A.

Finally, brothers and sisters, whatever is true, whatever is noble, whatever is right, whatever is pure, whatever is lovely, whatever is admirable—if anything is excellent or praiseworthy—think about such things.

—Philippians 4:8

Contents

Introduction

WHAT REALLY MATTERS IN education? Amid headlines about standardized tests, the United States lagging behind other countries, and the unreasonable costs of higher education, what really matters? Certainly any attempt to provide a definitive list of answers to such a question is problematic because we have a diversity of beliefs and values that inform individual philosophies and priorities in education. Nonetheless, we risk a more dangerous path if we do not grapple with this question. Meaning must not be abandoned for trends, unexamined policies and practices, or political positioning.

With this core conviction in mind, I offer this book as a discussion starter more than a treatise. I outline what I consider to be ten critical themes in contemporary education that largely transcend individual philosophies. While people will disagree on elements of these themes, the themes themselves represent large-scale conversations and concerns in modern education—concerns that reach a level of impact and importance that warrants a persistent, broad and national conversation. I will make the argument that these ten themes call for important reflections about deep and foundational issues that can help us create a more engaging, effective, humane, and authentic education system.

What are the most critical issues in education today? Answers to such a question are shaped by our own experiences, perspectives, and positions in the modern world of education. Nonetheless, this is a useful question. It challenges us to rank the many issues and challenges, allowing us to consider where we will devote our time, energy, and resources. This simple question is what is needed to navigate debates about policy on national and state levels, decisions about reform on all levels, as well as institution-specific strategy and planning. Whether we are lobbying for national policy or promoting a new program or practice in an individual school, we are wise to innovate from a place of clarity and purpose; and that means starting with a clear mission, vision, and set of values and goals. It means taking the time to consider the compelling *why* behind what we aspire to do. It calls for us to think about what we consider essential, important, and largely flexible in what we do in education. In other words, educational policy, reform, and innovation are better served by time spent looking inward, not simply looking at models and examples of others and imitating them.

While I undoubtedly present an incomplete list in this book, what follows are the ten issues that I will explore further as we progress through the text. I have sought to establish a list that is not married to any individual trend or innovation but still has immense power to inform which trends and innovations we pursue, how we pursue them, and how we evaluate their efficacy. These are largely focused on questions about the impact of learning and people more than the viability of a given organization or even professionals in the field of education. In other words, these are themes that transcend formal schooling structures, instead attending more broadly to education, the growth and development of learners in society.

Wasted Gifts, Talents, and Abilities

This is a broad topic, but it is one of the most troubling challenges in education today and it is the same challenge that has existed for millennia. Education, at its best, is about helping people discover, refine, and develop their gifts, talents, passions, and abilities; and then helping them discover how to use those gifts, talents, and abilities in ways that benefit others and themselves. There are too many places where this does not happen. Too many learners fall between the cracks. We have existing learning organizations where learners are part of the organization for years without having this journey of discovery.

This is also the motive behind some of the best education work today with regard to educational innovation—efforts in personalized and individualized education, recognizing that each person is unique, not just another widget. At the same time, it is within this theme that I also place the critical issue today of access and opportunity to education around the world. In the end, not pursuing educational access and opportunity is a terrible waste and loss of the gifts, talents, abilities, and passions of those people in different parts of the world.

Testing and Assessment

In itself, testing is not that critical of an issue, but today it is sometimes the tail that wags the dog. I included testing in this list because tests have too often become the focus. Testing should exist as a servant to the main goals of education. Whenever people start to build learning organizations and experiences around tests instead of designing tests to serve and amplify the organization's mission, vision, and values, we have a problem.

The other issue is that there are not many jobs in the world that pay people to be good test takers. What we want and need are assessment plans that bring out the best in people and organizations. As such, creativity and innovation around assessment might not sound interesting to people, but in this current age getting involved in the assessment domain is a valuable way to effect positive change in education.

Credentialism

This is a topic that gained attention in the 1970s,[1] but it is returning amid public criticism and questions about the value of a college degree. Credentialism is the concept that credentials sometimes become unnecessary and inequitable barriers to gainful employment and other aspects of society. A commonly given example is a job posting that lists a bachelor's degree as a requirement for applying, where if you assess the knowledge and skills actually needed for that job, there are likely many people without a bachelor's degree who could thrive in it. In those cases, we have created gated communities in the world of work that limit access and opportunity to otherwise qualified and hard-working people. The same thing is true with recent changes to the GED. While raising the bar seems like a good thing, it can also limit access in destructive ways.

Non-Cognitive Skills

Character, virtues, and non-cognitive skills have always been an important part of a person's growth and maturation, not only into adulthood but also throughout life. If we want to invest in aspects of education that have a demonstrable impact on the lives of individuals, their families, their communities, their places of work, and the entire world around them, we are wise to devote time and attention to how we can nurture these important elements that less frequently show up in a list of learning objectives for a course or goals for a formal program. We are talking about traits like grit, courage, conscientiousness, integrity, personal ownership, the capacity to postpone gratification, collaboration skills, the ability to plan and prioritize, and many others.

Also within this category, I look to two traits that I am drawn to exploring and addressing, namely curiosity and the love of learning. Ultimately, if we are able to nurture or awaken such traits in people, then we will have made great progress in creating a culture of learning that will benefit countless people. What happens

1. See Illich, *Disabling Professions*.

when we begin to design learning organizations that are rich in a culture of curiosity and a love of learning? What are the benefits to the learners in such communities and to society as a whole?

Agency

While related to the last theme, I give this such a high priority that it deserves a category of its own. Human agency is about the capacity for people to understand that they have choices that impact their lives. I use it in contrast to a fatalistic or deterministic mindset. It is recognizing that the choices we make have a large and lasting impact on what happens in our lives. Yes, there are many things beyond our control, but nurturing a sense of agency makes a difference in our outlook on life, our engagement in civic life, and our approach to personal and professional activities. A lack of agency is consistently detrimental to the well-being of individuals, families, communities, and nations.

Purpose and Meaning

Similar to agency, when purpose and meaning are absent, despair and depression are soon to follow. One of the most dangerous ideas in society and education is the idea that there is no purpose or meaning to a person's life or to life in general. We can't pretend that we are able to somehow create educational contexts that are neutral about matters of purpose and meaning. They are fundamental to the educational endeavor. Without them, education itself loses purpose and meaning. As such, we must resist educational and societal efforts that insist on simply deconstructing anything and everything around us, leaving it dismantled and broken. When we deconstruct, we have a responsibility to build. When and if we deconstruct, we must join others in reconstructing something that is true, good, and beautiful.

Education is often about teaching people to critique, but that must be accompanied with nurturing the capacity to create, to discover and embrace the purpose and meaning in the world around us. While world religions have pointed to such a premise for millennia, this is also supported by contemporary research across multiple disciplines.

The Digital Divide

Among all these other big ideas, does the digital divide really have a proper place? Isn't it better suited for a conversation with a group of people who work in information technology? While that might have been arguable in the past, we now live in a digital age, an increasingly connected and digital world. Lacking access, confidence, or the capacity to leverage the digital or connected world puts people at a societal disadvantage. Our connections with people, content, and communities that were once central to most people's lives have becoming increasingly digitized.

It is hard to even be an informed citizen in an upcoming election today without being connected. The same is true for trying to find a job and then getting that job, or learning about resources for yourself or your family. As such, this remains a major issue in education. This is about more than not having hardware or an Internet connection. It is also about having the character, competencies, confidence, and convictions to take advantage of that connection.

Edu-Technopoly

In 1993, Neil Postman published a provocative and influential book entitled, *Technopoly*. In this book he opened many of our eyes to the reality that all technology, even that which is so familiar that we do not think of it as technology, has affordances and limitations. There are things gained and lost, winners and losers. The same is true with educational technology, and we are now in an era where educational technology is front and center in education.

As George Siemens wrote about in a September 2015 blog post, there is a danger of educational technology shaping us more than us shaping the technology.[2] This is a persistent caution in the media ecology movement and from many scholars. It is partly why I devoted several years studying and learning from Luddite and low-tech movements (like the Amish) in contemporary society. They provide an important balance and perspective in this technological age. "We shape our tools and afterwards our tools shape us."[3] And as Sherry Turkle lamented (and cautioned):

> We know that once computers connected us to each other, once we became tethered to the network, we really didn't need to keep computers busy. They keep us busy. It is as though we have become their killer app. As a friend of mine put it in a moment of pique, "We don't do our e-mail; our e-mail does us." We talk about "spending" hours on e-mail, but we, too, are being spent. Niels Bohr suggests that the opposite of a "deep truth" is a truth no less profound. As we contemplate online life, it helps to keep this in mind.[4]

We live in a technological age and there is no going back from this. Yet, more than ever, it is imperative that we shed light on the affordances and limitations of the age, nurturing a critical and creative eye to such a world, and finding ways to elevate and amplify what it means to be human instead of simply letting the technology redefine humanity for us.

Vocation and Good Work

This is not a claim that schools should be entirely focused on job preparation, but work is an important part of life, and education (not just schooling) is an essential part of preparing people to get and do work with excellence and character. Work can be rewarding, fulfilling, honorable, and impactful. It is not just what we do

2. Siemens, "Adios EdTech."
3. Culken, "Schoolman's Guide," 70.
4. Turkle, *Alone Together*, 279.

but how we do it, as so wonderfully explained in Gardner and Csikszentmihalyi's book *Good Work*.[5]

As James H. Douglas Jr. is quoted as saying, "A good job is more than just a paycheck. A good job fosters independence and discipline, and contributes to the health of the community. A good job is a means to provide for the health and welfare of your family, to own a home, and save for retirement."[6] I can think of no better way to highlight the role of education as a path to good work than to come back to the words of Dr. Martin Luther King Jr.:

> What I'm saying to you this morning, my friends, even if it falls your lot to be a street sweeper, go on out and sweep streets like Michelangelo painted pictures; sweep streets like Handel and Beethoven composed music; sweep streets like Shakespeare wrote poetry; [*go ahead*] sweep streets so well that all the host of heaven and earth will have to pause and say, "Here lived a great street sweeper who swept his job well."[7]
>
> "No work is insignificant. All labor that uplifts humanity has dignity and importance and should be undertaken with painstaking excellence."[8]

Among its many roles, formal and informal education serves to help people experience and embrace such truths about work and the more historic concept of vocation or calling. It is a concept with a long history in religious traditions, recognizing the sacred nature of our many roles in life ranging from family and community roles to the roles that result in a paycheck. Meaningful education reform of our age calls for us to remember these important perspectives on work and vocation.

5. Gardner et al., *Good Work*.

6. Quoted from http://experiencecle.com/2015/06/career-development-the-cle-way/.

7. King, "Three Dimensions," para. 11.

8. King, quoted from Sequeira, "MLK Quote of the Week."

Truth, Beauty, and Goodness

I am not a classicist when it comes to education, although I have learned much and am greatly influenced by classical perspectives on education, even as many would likely label me as some blend of educational existentialist, constructivist, connectivist, and progressivist. However, because of what I have already written about meaning and purpose, I am persistently drawn back to three classical foundations for education, namely the pursuit and study of truth, beauty, and goodness.

When we lose sight of this in education, our learning organizations lose much of what makes them distinctive and enriching in some of the deepest and most substantive ways. As I follow educational trends in K–12 and higher education within the United States and around the world I see the greatest hope where these three classical elements are alive and well. They help to shape the vision of the K–12 and higher education institutions, occupying the thoughts of teacher and learner alike. For insights on this topic we can look to contemporary reflections of educators ranging from Martha Nussbaum to Howard Gardner, or we can return to more historical insights of thinkers like Plato.

There are certainly more than just these ten themes, but the ones that I have selected represent what I consider to be some of the most critical and pressing issues. They represent ideas that can lead to good and important reform, and promising work in educational innovation. I invite you to join me as we delve more deeply into them in the forthcoming pages.

The ideas in this text come from over two decades of writing, speaking and reflection on these subjects. While much of this book is original content, other aspects have been drawn and revised from other works. When appropriate, I cite other works, with the exception of ideas that came from rough-draft blog posts or presentations without published proceedings over the years. If an idea came from some formal publishing route in an article, monograph, or earlier book, you will find citations and references to those works. Nonetheless, I am excited to offer this work as a refinement, collection, and curation of many ideas drawn from diverse areas of study and across many educational contexts. It is my hope and prayer that you, as the reader, find it thought provoking, helping you to grapple with and engage in conversations with others about critical issues in contemporary education.

1

Wasted Talents, Gifts, and Abilities

IN A 2015 PRESENTATION at the Twenty-First Century Learning Conference in Hong Kong, Mark Treadwell, a leading thinker on how our knowledge about the human brain can and should shape school, argued that schools of the past were good at convincing the majority of students that they were not smart. In fact, Treadwell argued, one of the roles of school in the past was to convince 80 percent of the students that they were not very smart, leading them to be content pursuing less complex jobs that were necessary to keep the economy going. It is not like school leaders or classroom teachers set out to make young people think that they are not smart, but Treadwell argues that this was and is the outcome based upon the system that we have in place. Going into the future, he argued that we need to convince 80 percent of the students that they are smart because the jobs and tasks required of people in the future will demand as much. I'd like to argue for moving that 80 percent to 100 percent, not on the basis of future job demands, but based upon a desire to no longer leave room for wasted gifts, talents, and abilities in our schools and communities.

Whether you agree with Mark Treadwell's claim that schools convince 80 percent of the students that they are not smart, tempering their ambition and preparing them for the mass workforce, his comments get at the heart of the single most critical educational issue of our time. That issue is the wasted gifts, talents, and abilities of young people in our schools. Allow me to explain.

Perhaps you've seen the cartoon where there is a long line of animals: a monkey, penguin, seal, fish, elephant, bird, and a dog. Then there is a man sitting behind a desk saying, "For a fair selection everybody has to take the same exam: please climb that tree."[1] Welcome to the common mindset behind some of the most dominant educational policy discussions of the twenty-first century.

Years ago I talked with the superintendent of a respected school district about the promise and possibility of designing a charter school in the district focused upon project-based learning, personalized learning, and helping students discover their calling. At first this superintendent was excited and welcomed a follow-up meeting. Amid the tyranny of the urgent in our schedules, we didn't follow up for several months. When I reached out about a lunch appointment, I learned that this superintendent's viewpoint seemed to have changed. She said that she was happy to have lunch, but that she didn't have much interest in a project-based charter school. She explained her change of mind with a single sentence: "I've been thinking about this, and I tend to think that what is good for one student is good for all students."

To be fair, we never had a follow-up conversation about this, but this single sentence left me baffled. Is there a different way to read it? What is good for one is good for all? Whether or not it was the intent of the superintendent, there are plenty of people today who advocate for a national reform in education and strive to find the model, method, and universal set of standards that can be applied across the board for the benefit of everyone. The problem is that there is no such thing as a universal model, method, or set of standards that is best for all students.

There are some largely universal principles (like the idea that feedback is important in learning), but principles leave room for diverse applications. None have proven that there is a standard template that will bring the best out in all learners. There is no universal set of academic standards that, if met, will assure that

---

1. This illustration has been shared and retold in slightly different forms countless times over the years. The earliest reference I have found is in a 1996 article, Brown, "Let's Make It Fair."

each learner thrives and is a positive and contributing member of society. Standards, models, methods and frameworks are helpful, but they are not universal when it comes to designing learning organizations.

Having a universal model for education is the educational equivalent of claiming to have a single magic pill that treats all ailments and conditions. Yes, there are some largely universal principles. Eat well. Exercise regularly. Get adequate sleep. Yet, even with those three elements, there seems to be plenty of evidence that different people benefit from different types of exercise, different diets, and maybe even different sleeping habits and personalized medications.

People have different gifts, talents, abilities, propensities, life experiences, challenges, opportunities, and ultimately different callings in life. This means that they will benefit from different learning opportunities and experiences. There are good times for shared learning experiences, but what happens when the schooling options available to a student come from a limited perspective on which gifts and abilities should be celebrated and strengthened? Plenty of good can come from a core of shared learning experiences, but we also need to draw out, affirm, and amplify the differences among learners.

At the foundation of every learning organization is a set of values, beliefs, and convictions about education. People don't agree on these matters. As such, I am not ready to force my philosophy of education on the rest of the world, nor do I want that done to me. I might make persistent and passionate arguments in favor of my positions, but at the end of the day we are better off finding ways to leave room for diverse perspectives on education to live alongside one another. That means a universal commitment to diverse learning environments—to choices.

"Parents have a prior right to choose the kind of education that shall be given to their children."[2] That is a direct quote from the Universal Declaration of Human Rights. I realize that readers

2. UN General Assembly, "Universal Declaration of Human Rights," art. 26.

of this book hold to diverse viewpoints on this document in general, but this is a portion that I wholeheartedly support. Some have argued that children ultimately belong to the state. Others, including myself, argue that the family unit is a fundamental, foundational unit in society.

The fact that there is disagreement about this re-entered the broader public discourse in 2013 when Melissa Harris-Perry argued that "we have to break through our kind of private idea that kids belong to their parents or kids belong to their families and recognize that kids belong to whole communities."[3] The concerning part in her comment is that she somehow seemed to miss or disregard that there is a real and historical debate about these claims.[4]

And this is just one of many philosophical differences about education and children. There are many more when we start diving into curriculum and the ultimate aims of education. Given such differences, it seems reasonable that we stick with and maybe even expand a diversity of models and approaches to education. In such a climate, arguing for a universal model is a disregard for these important differences.

Each person is a unique creation, full of potential, too precious to disregard intentionally or unintentionally (but as a result of institutional structures). Our pursuit in education should be to provide an excellent education for all. What is good for one is good for all, and what is good for one is a learning experience that best supports, celebrates, and launches that one person into a life of significance, meaning, and impact. That doesn't happen with a one-size-fits-all approach to education.

I do not question the value of a common body of knowledge to some extent, but that is different from arguing for the same type of education for every child driven by the same tests. True equity, access, and opportunity will come from educational choice and a diversity of educational options. This is why I continue to argue

3. James, "MSNBC: We Have to Break Through," para. 3.

4. For a thorough exploration of the matter, check out Amy Gutman's 1987 book, *Democratic Education*.

that a great strength of the United States educational landscape is the rich diversity. On the K–12 level I'm referring to legacy public, public magnet, public charter, independent, parochial, home-schooling, unschooling, world schooling, project-based learning schools, game-based learning schools, STEM academies, bilingual schools, democratic schools, Waldorf schools, Montessori schools, and a myriad of others. On the university level I'm referring to everything from small liberal arts colleges to state universities, blended and online options to technical and community colleges, public to private and faith-based, elite schools to a wonderfully interesting collection of alternative schools, even (maybe especially) the self-directed and non-college options available today.[5]

In 2015 there were several critiques of Arne Duncan, former US Secretary of Education, for sending his children to the University of Chicago Lab Schools. Part of the critique was that he was sending his kids to a school that does not align with many of his educational reform efforts as Secretary of Education. I appreciate that critique, but from another perspective I commend him for selecting a school that he thinks is the best fit for his kids. Now all we need to do is to pursue more national and state policies that make sure such choice is more widely available to the rest of the families in the country. Duncan knows that you don't test an elephant by how well it can climb a tree, and he knows that the same thing is true when it comes to finding the right fit between a student and a school.

Signs of a Self-Absorbed Culture?

Isn't this just another sign of our increasingly self-absorbed culture? Students wanting everything their way instead of sucking it up and doing the work? I've talked to more than a few people who think as much, but there is another way of looking at this issue. This is about a more personalized and customized approach

5. One noteworthy example is Wayfinding Academy, a startup college in Oregon that was launched by a crowd-funding campaign in 2015 and focuses upon helping students discover and build upon their passions.

to education. It is a recognition that people are different and we can best celebrate and maximize those differences by matching the student with the best-fit school. This isn't about catering to every whim and preference of a person. It is instead a perspective that doesn't want to see a single student go to waste, one that aspires for learners to discover their unique contributions to the world. This is ultimately not about self-service, but it is about best positioning students to discover how they can live a rich and fulfilling life that benefits themselves and the people around them. And while some argue that focusing on STEM in our schools is the key to winning some international economic competition, I continue to defend the position that the nation and world will be better off if we invest in maximizing the potential of each person instead of sifting out those who don't fit the STEM mold. In fact, by choosing a more personalized approach we may find that we gain more traction than ever on everything from crime reduction to workforce and economic development.

People are concerned about waste in education. Scan the headlines about university education and people are incredibly concerned about wasted financial resources and the cost of college. Look at debates on the K–12 level and we read about wasted investment in unused technology and concerns about teachers. Some argue that teachers need to be held more accountable, while others argue that they need to be more celebrated, supported, and empowered. I don't deny the importance of these topics, and we want to spend ample time addressing these challenges and working on them. Nonetheless, at the end of the day, it comes back to the students.

A Lesson from Buckminster Fuller

Buckminster Fuller was an eccentric but unquestionably brilliant twentieth-century inventor. While he rejected the title of futurist, the vision represented in many of his inventions reached decades into the future. His work continues to inspire new innovations and inventions. Earlier in his life he experienced a crisis that, according to his own lectures and writings, led him to contemplate taking his own life. As he stood by the shore of Lake Michigan in Chicago, he considered swimming out into the ice-cold water to the point of no return.[6]

Before entering the water, he had an experience that changed the course of his life. One thing that he realized through this experience is the idea that each person in the world is in a position to contribute something that no other person will ever be able to contribute. Each person has a unique combination of experiences, gifts, talents, abilities, proclivities, strengths, limitations, passions, and interests. In that sense each person is irreplaceable. No other person has ever or will ever bring that same combination into the world. From this epiphany, Fuller spent the rest of life conducting an experiment.

> I sought to use myself as my scientific "guinea pig" in a lifelong experiment designed to discover what—if anything—a healthy young male human of average size, experience and capability with an economically dependent wife and newborn child, starting without capital or any kind of wealth, cash savings, account monies, credit, or university degree, could effectively do that could not be done by great nations or great private enterprise to lastingly improve the physical protection and support of all human lives, at the same time removing undesirable restraints and improving individual initiatives of any and all humans aboard our planet Earth.[7]

It is only in 2012 that I learned about Buckminster Fuller. Since then I've had a consistent diet of his work, writing, and the many recordings of his lectures. I don't agree with or understand everything that he said or wrote, but I can't help but be inspired by the sense of purpose that shaped his life and work. This brings me back to the one thing that we can't afford to waste in education.

Fuller believed that every person had something valuable to offer the world. If that is true, then the greatest mistake of our

6. Sieden, *Buckminster Fuller's Universe*, 87–89.
7. Fuller, *Critical Path*, 124.

learning organizations would be to function as if nurturing commonalities is the most important aspect of schooling, or to set up systems that celebrate certain gifts, abilities, and accomplishments while disregarding or minimizing others. Standardization is about commonalities and about highlighting when a student does not fit the mold or make the grade. It is about labeling people and paying special attention to the "A-grade" talent, as if the hidden or muffled talents of the others are somehow less valuable.

Communities of Potential

Schools are communities of people with potential. The goal is to celebrate, discover, refine, and develop that potential in each person. While the history of American public education is, according to some, about nurturing commonalities, I contend that making that the foundation of education is not only dangerous, but wasteful. As the world becomes increasingly aware of the environmental dangers of waste and pollution, this is a perfect time for our learning organizations to become just as focused upon eradicating another type of waste—the waste of the unique potential in each person.

As such, we are best positioned when we build an education system that nurtures important commonalities while also helping people discover and develop their uniqueness. There are times to nurture and develop commonalities. The things that we share can be an important bond in a community and culture. Yet, building an entire educational system on that is an industrial exercise. It is mass production, turning education into one-size-fits-all factories. For education to have the greatest impact, it must teach and celebrate commonalities while placing just as much (maybe more) attention on the uncommon that is present in each person.

Most learning organizations are not set up for such a task. For a long time, schools have been focused upon teaching groups of individuals, not teaching individuals. While there are plenty of great educators who find ways to nurture individual strengths, the existing system is not well-suited for this. We have a system that wastes the gifts and abilities of young people.

The national conversation about education reform continues to pay little attention to this perspective on education. Those national debates are more centered on testing, standards, school and teacher accountability, and educational access. Yet, even when the value of each individual is important part of the conversation, it consistently fails to make the headlines or show up in policy work.

The Good News

The good news is that there are schools that embrace this vision. I've seen it in independent schools like Acton Academy in Austin, Texas, where project-based learning is commonplace, personalized learning dominates, and each student is invited to go on a Hero's Journey. It is alive at KM Global, a project-based charter school in Wales, Wisconsin, where students complete a series of large student-driven interdisciplinary projects throughout their high school experience. It is alive in schools like Amazing Grace and Renton Prep in Seattle, Washington, an elementary school and high school that invite students to make use of their unique gifts through world-class inquiry-based learning, project-based learning, and participating in a learning community that values things like creativity, humility, resolve, interdependency, and simplicity.[8] It is alive in many Montessori schools around the world, not to mention countless teachers and school leaders who are awakening to the fact that school must be a place that honors, celebrates, and nurtures the uniqueness of each learner.

---

8. See http://www.rentonprep.org for more information about this school.

2

Testing and Assessment

TESTING IS NOT A critical life skill. People who are great at taking tests do not thrive in work or family more than others. There is no strong evidence that great test takers make better presidents, parents, teachers, doctors, lawyers, or anything else. Tests and assessments are servants of a greater cause, and tests and assessment have become a critical issue in education because of their misuse. This topic becomes critical when such facts get lost or overlooked amid debates about quality, education reform, accountability, and big data in education. We will not test or assess our way through education's greatest challenges, but if we are not careful, tests and assessment can delay or subvert our progress.

The Case of the General Educational Development Test

As a way to illustrate the impact of tests in education, consider the case of a single test used for students seeking their GED (General Education Development) diploma. On January 2, 2014, a new version of the GED test was published. What changed and what are the results? Let's answer the second question first. According to an NPR article, the number of graduates declined by 85 percent since the new test. This is a drop from over 400,000 people passing the test in 2012 to less than 60,000 in 2014.[1]

---

1. Turner and Kamentz, "Sizable Decrease," para. 1.

- They doubled the price from sixty dollars to one hundred twenty dollars and partnered with the for-profit Pearson to administer the test.

- A credit card is the standard form of payment (although they have other options as well).

- It is now a computer-based test.

They changed the standards upon which the test was built, aligning it with the Common Core State Standards.[2]

Advocates for the new test argue that it more accurately represents the standards expected of high schools for a traditional diploma and employers seeking to hire people with a diploma or its equal. Simply looking at the four new features above, there appears to be more to the story.

Consider Neil Postman's important questions for evaluating new technologies or innovations. Who are the winners and losers?[3] "What sort of institutions acquire special economic and political power because of technological change?"[4] How might we answer that question for this new test? Certainly the company giving the test has something to gain since this is a new revenue stream for the company. What about employers? Are employers raving about how GED graduates of 2014 are so much more effective on the job than those who earned their GED in previous years? What about the fact that so many fewer GED graduates are available? There may be some employers out there whose business can handle simply leaving positions vacant until a larger percentage of people can pass the new test and therefore be qualified for employment. Or they can just hire people without a GED or diploma. More likely is that people who pursued the GED after January 2014 but failed the test are just out of luck. They may be just as qualified as someone who took the test a year earlier, but they get passed over for the job

2. Ibid., para. 3.

3. Postman, "Five Things We Need to Know," 3.

4. Postman, "Technology and Society," at 1:54 in part 5 of the YouTube posting.

because they don't meet the minimum requirements, even if those requirements were not necessary to do the job.

That brings us to thinking about who the losers are with this new test as well as many other tests. With regard to the newer GED, the people who didn't pass are an obvious group that fits into this category. But before I even get to the test itself, I'll start with the payment system. When the test was first released, a credit card was the seemingly standard and expected method, although they did accommodate other options. Yet, even the payment process has been complicated with this new test.[5] Why put any unnecessary barriers in front of students? How is this new payment system designed to represent the best interest of these students?

Now to the impact of failing this test. If people don't pass this new GED, they have fewer opportunities available to them. What happens to people without a high school diploma or GED? While we can respect the caution of confusing correlation with causation, people without a GED or diploma are more likely to be unemployed, imprisoned, and/or stuck in a cycle of poverty.[6] We can dismiss these realities by explaining how we must maintain high standards and "academic rigor" through this new GED, but this is not about maintaining. They raised the bar, and to the best of my knowledge they did so without any substantive body of research as to how this will produce greater social good, better benefit the well-being of people in GED programs, or even benefit the employers of people with a high school diploma or GED. Simply saying that these new standards will produce more capable employees is not adequate. Show me the evidence. Look at the types of skills required of people in jobs with a prerequisite of a GED or high school diploma but no higher credential. Show, through a workforce skills assessment, that the old test inadequately prepared people for those jobs, while the new test does. That will at least help me reconsider my position.

This is too massive of a shift of to just guess or even lean on what some claim to be common sense. There are too many

5. See http://www.gedtestingservice.com/educators/payments.

6. Bridgeland et al., "Silent Epidemic," i.

complexities, too many people's life situations at stake, and too little hard data to support the decision. If we really wanted to pursue this development without such massive potential negative implications, I have another simple suggestion, one that was overlooked or disregarded. Why not design a test that is based upon both the 2013 and 2014 standards, giving those who meet or exceed the 2014 standards an honors GED and the others a standards GED? This way we would be raising the bar without using a nation of GED students as guinea pigs.

Yet, that is not what people did. They changed everything overnight and, at the time of this publication, have done little to address some of the potential harm inflicted on people and society. As a result, some states abandoned this test as a requirement for a GED, opting for alternatives and deviating from what was previously a standard GED test for over sixty years. I guess if you are doubling the price for the test, you can handle losing half your customers.

When the Testing Tail Wags the Educational Dog

There are likely many other considerations that influenced the decision to change the GED, but this example illustrates a critical issue in education, namely the problem of letting the testing tail wag the educational dog. Tests are tools. They exist to serve the students and educators. One of the main reasons they exist today is to help measure student growth and learning. However, we also use them as ways to maintain standards for obtaining a credential or entering into a new profession or field. A problem arises when we confuse these two distinct uses of tests or we fail to consider the larger implications of how we use tests in a given context or for a given purpose.

Within most schools, tests are often used a means of generating a grade for students, but their greatest value as a teaching tool is not to document performance, but to provide a measure of learning. Note that I am using word "test" in the broadest sense. Consider the example of tests in a medical context. I have a blood test and the results provide the doctor and myself with insights into my health. The results may indicate that there are specific concerns and challenges that warrant further attention, treatment, or lifestyle changes. The results may also provide positive feedback, affirming my current lifestyle habits. Imagine what would happen if those tests were instead primarily used to give me a health grade that resulted in determining whether I get access to something else in life. If I score low on the blood tests, I get a D for health and that record serves to haunt and hinder me for the future. While there are certainly times when health evaluations are used to determine a person's fitness for a given job or activity, that is not their primary use. I contend that the same perspective is useful in formal education.

Tests are powerful and useful measures of student learning and performance, but not just to document and update what will become a permanent record, and will be used to open or close opportunities for people in the future. What if we instead created a context in schools where tests truly were used with the main goal of helping each learner make substantive progress? Tests would be less about documenting and more about monitoring and helping people grow and learn.

One challenge is that the contemporary testing landscape, especially in K–12 education, has become increasingly political. Tests in the public are discussed more in terms of measuring school performance and less in terms of how they help individuals learn and progress. There are many examples where tests are used to monitor individual progress, but the larger public discourse today does not include substantive dialogue about this aspect. Instead, test scores are looked at in the aggregate and used to create scorecards for schools or to assess (or critique) the quality of overall education systems. These may well be valid uses of tests, but I contend that education reform efforts will be better served by shifting to an emphasis upon tests and assessments that help individual learners.

What would this look like? Consider tests as tools for feedback, even instances where many tests and assessments do not contribute points to an overall grade. Rather, they are treated more like learning tools. This goes counter to the way many people think about the proper use of tests. Critics might contend that this decreases the academic rigor of a class or learning context, or that it reduces student motivation. Yet, this points to one of the challenges with tests in many learning contexts. They become a means to cover up more fundamental problems in the learning context: problems about lack of engagement, motivation, and learner interest. Furthermore, using tests as the primary means of promoting academic rigor or challenge also represents a lack of creativity or effort in the overall design of rich and engaging learning environments. If the typical expertise in the education profession has not caught up with the research on the design of quality learning experiences, student motivation, and student engagement, then testing is simply covering up this more significant and fundamental problem.

The Benefits of Emphasizing Formative Assessment

Assessment in education (and testing as a form or a subcategory of assessment) exists to measure learning and abilities. From an instructional designer's perspective, I often describe formative assessment (in contrast to summative assessment) in a particular way. I'm not sure where I first heard it, but some say that formative assessment is the check-up at the doctor, where summative assessment is the autopsy. Formative assessment is about gaining feedback that can help one adjust the teaching and learning process while it is still happening. It is about getting helpful data that can lead to changes in behavior, strategies, methods, level of effort, or something else that has a good chance of improving performance or learning.

Such data need not come from a traditional test. In fact, tests are often limited in their ability to provide the most helpful data. Consider the following explanation from Alfie Kohn:

> Once the teacher has figured out the extent to which students' thinking is becoming more sophisticated and where gaps still exist, there's obviously no need to reduce

the conclusion to a summary letter (B) or a number (84) or a label that functions just like a letter or number but allows us to pretend we're doing something different ("exceeds expectations"). Instead a qualitative description or evaluation can be offered in narrative form—or, better yet, as apart of a dialogue during a meting with students or parents.[7]

If there is a clear learning goal or objective, then formative assessments can help the teacher to see how a given student is progressing toward that goal, and what the student does or does not understand at a given moment. They also play an important role for the learner so that she develops the ability to use formative assessments to track her own understanding, and to use that information to decide how and what to do next in the learning process. This ability for self-reflection, self-monitoring, and self-assessment is, after all, an important life skill.

When there is a growing reliance upon tests and formal measures as the dominant form of formative (not just summative) assessment, we begin to lose the primary purpose of formative assessment, not to mention creating and increasing unnecessary anxiety for learners. This risks minimizing the power and value of the many quick and less formal formative assessments that provide rich guidance and insight for teachers and learners: admission and exit tickets, think/pair/share activities, class discussions, simple checklists of observations during class, self-assessment checklists and rubrics, learning journals/logs, feedback from adaptive learning software, etc.

These can be done multiple times a day with minimal effort. Narrative forms of assessment, for example, provide insight that one will rarely gain from something like the MAPS test, which boasts that, "You'll have essential information about what each student knows and is ready to learn within 24 hours."[8] Such a test can be a helpful tool, but the informal formative assessments within a

7. Bower and Thomas, *De-Testing and De-Grading Schools*, 3.

8. Northwest Evaluation Association, "Measure Student Progress with MAP."

class help teachers get the know learners on a level of detail that is not yet possible with the more formal tests. They also help learners get to know themselves. They do what qualitative research can do and what quantitative research can't: provide rich descriptions that help surface underlying reasons about what inspires students, scares them, encourages them, and baffles them. They give nearly real-time data that can help teachers and learners adjust.

Another concern is that many of the more formal tools used for formative assessment focus upon the deficiency model of education. "Find out the gaps and deficiencies of learners so that you can fill them," some might reason. In many contexts, that is good and essential to help students find success. In the process, it risks putting a hefty focus upon what students are unable to do, which is helpful information but not the entire picture. The deficiency model of education argues that students will best learn if we point out their weaknesses and devote the majority of their time to fixing those weaknesses. There is a time for this. This might result in gains, but in some instances it might do so at the cost of failing to nurturing the passions and strengths of the learner (not to mention the learner's motivation). While weaknesses that hold us back must be addressed, there is another vision for learning, strength-based education, which seeks to discover a learner's strengths and spend significant time helping the learner to lean into those strengths, building upon them, strengthening them even more. Along the way, they can address some of the weaker areas as well.

Consider this first sentence in the Wikipedia entry for formative assessment: "Formative assessment or diagnostic testing is a range of formal and informal assessment procedures employed by teachers during the learning process to change teaching and learning activities to improve student attainment."[9] If you look up "diagnostic test," you get this: "A diagnostic test is any kind of medical test performed to aid in the diagnosis or detection of disease."[10]

9. Wikipedia, "Formative Assessment," para. 1, https://en.wikipedia.org/wiki/Formative_assessment.

10. Wikipedia, "Diagnostic Test," para. 1, https://en.wikipedia.org/wiki/Diagnostic_test.

Where the formative assessment article dealt with teaching and learning contexts, the diagnostic test page deals with medical testing. This is a crowd-sourced encyclopedia and my role as a digital citizen is to figure out how to contribute to addressing this problem with the articles. However, I couldn't help but reflect on the irony of the current (as of writing this chapter) way that diagnostic testing is represented. Diagnostic testing is about "diagnosing and detecting disease"! There is a risk that this is precisely how the testing culture is leading us to think about student learning. A student who performs "poorly" has a "learning disease" that requires a treatment or intervention. Again, this can be a helpful perspective in some instances, but it can be destructive when the entire schooling model commits to this as the sole or dominant perspective.

The use of formal (often norm-referenced) tests for formative assessment also has the limitation of measuring that which can be easily and quickly measured, looking past important aspects of the learning process and experience that are difficult to get at with an automated grading tool. There is room for such tests, even as formative assessments, but it will be a significant loss for our students if we allow the term "formative assessment" to be redefined in the K–12 education vernacular as dealing primarily with the use of formal tests.

There is a solid body of literature that supports the power of formative assessment and feedback.[11] Learning experiences typically have at least four key components. There is a learning goal or objective. There is a plan to help students reach that goal or objective. There is a means of determining whether students meet the goal or objective. Then there is a plan to monitor student progress toward meeting the learning goal or objective. Notice that two of these four key elements are about assessment.

We can apply these to almost any learning environment, formal or informal, in school or independent of school. Consider something like learning to ride a bike. The goal is to be able to ride a bike without falling over or needing the help of someone else. The strategy might be to start with training wheels, then to remove

11. Andrade and Cizek, *Handbook of Formative Assessment.*

the training wheels but have the support of a parent's hand on the back of the seat. Every so often the parent removes his or her hand from the seat to see if the young person is balancing enough to make it without assistance. The parent might also provide some tips or feedback along the way. In addition, the young person is monitoring himself or herself, getting a feel for whether or not they are getting closer to the goal. Ultimately, the "test" happens when the learner has the competence and confidence to try a more extended ride without a parent's help. Notice how much feedback and assessment is embedded into that learning experience. There is ongoing self-assessment, formative teacher assessment, and there is hardly a moment that passes without feedback. Incredibly, all of this learning takes place for millions of children around the world without implementing a single standardized, high-stakes assessment, and without a detailed analysis of the aggregate data about emerging bike riders around the world.

While learning to ride a bike is not the same as learning about American history, learning the scientific method, or becoming a proficient reader or writer, they all share the presence of these four elements of a learning experience, with a heavy dose of feedback and assessment naturally integrated into the process. Hundreds of millions can learn to ride bikes with such formative feedback and assessment, and the same thing is true for learning pretty much anything. We do not need massive investments in high stakes tests to achieve grand learning goals for our organizations. It is not a major factor in improved learning.

The sooner we recognize this fact, the sooner we can embrace the forms of assessment that really matter for student learning. The sooner we see the contemporary testing culture as a distraction from great learning experience, the sooner we can reinvest much of that time, energy, and expense into the aspects of teaching and learning that really matter for learners of all types and ages.

Signs of a Shifting National Conversation

The good news is that, as of 2015, we witnessed the beginnings of a national conversation about cutting back on testing, enhancing learning, and maybe once and for all slaying the testing dragon in American education (or at least taming it, which is probably more difficult). As I wrote in the introduction, there is hope when people stop building learning organizations and experiences around tests, and instead start designing tests to serve and amplify the organization's mission, vision, and values.

For the first time in a long time (at least in such an explicit way), we got to hear support for the same general idea from the White House. On Saturday, October 24, 2015, President Obama shared a short (less than two minutes) video. In his concluding remarks, he highlighted a three-point guide for testing in schools:

1. Our kids should only take tests that are worth taking.

2. Tests should enhance teaching and learning.

3. Tests should give an all-around look at how our students and schools are doing.[12]

Then he finished with a couple of noteworthy quotes:

> Because learning is about so much more than filling in the right bubble. . . .
>
> . . . to make sure that our kids are enjoying learning.[13]

This is a fine start to a national conversation. And while these three principles are a solid starting point, we have much work to do beyond them. There is ample room for people to look at these three principles and contend that what is happening across the country is already complying with the President's charge. While many of us would challenge such a claim (and I think the evidence would be on our side), it isn't clear for all. For too many people, standardized

---

12. Quoted from the video posted on the White House Facebook page at https://www.facebook.com/WhiteHouse/videos/10153858935674238/.

13. Ibid.

tests and traditional tests in general are synonymous with high academic standards, academic rigor, and challenging students to high levels of performance. As such, if we want to address the testing problem, it is going to require a design revolution as much or more than efforts on the policy level.

As far as I am concerned, the problem with testing in schools is caused by a lack of creativity and depth about how to design rich, engaging, high-impact cultures of learning . . . that and pressures around demonstrating progress, even if in less holistic ways, to policymakers and external agencies. A culture of earning still dominates in the American school system. Teachers sometimes still lean on tests and quizzes for classroom management. Student questions are often focused on what they need to know for the test instead of what they want or need to learn for life, personal interest, or the achievement of an important goal. People looking at schools from the outside are too often focused on test scores as a sign that something good is happening. As such, a design revolution focused on school culture is a key to this shift, and that has to start with examining our core convictions about the purpose of school and building from there.

This statement from President Obama came amid large-scale moves toward more testing in schools across the country. This happened to demonstrate adequate yearly progress, to show whether students are meeting state standards and/or the Common Core State Standards (CCSS), and because big data is a growing part of the education landscape and traditional multiple choice tests are easier for the quantitatively minded to analyze across large populations. Such testing is not used because the research shows us how impactful it is for creating high-impact and engaging learning communities. It doesn't exist to help individual students so much as to help people analyze large pools of students or to speed the grading process for teachers.

Yet, even before No Child Left Behind, CCSS, and big data, we had a problem with such tests in our schools. For a long time, teachers have turned to true/false, multiple choice, and matching tests to keep students "motivated" and compliant, but even more so to make grading easier and bearable for the teachers. We can learn plenty about student progress through detailed rubrics, rich narrative feedback, and oral assessments, devising a triangulation of feedback from various sources, real-time coaching, and amid immersive and authentic projects. We can do all of that without touching a single traditional test. In addition, we know that these other forms of feedback and assessment generate more authentic and engaging learning environments.

In addition to all these strategies, we are on the verge of a learning analytics revolution, where computer-augmented learning experiences track student learning, behaviors, and progress in real-time. Formative and summative assessments merge as one in this new space, giving the student valuable instant feedback, giving teachers and others insight on student progress, and allowing others to analyze these data across large populations, all without testing. There is no need for traditional tests in this new world of learning.

I can't think of a better way to end this chapter than with a substantively (two key words changed) revised quote from Bertrand Russell: "It is possible that [education] is on the threshold of a golden age; but, if so, it will be necessary first to slay the dragon that guards the door, and this dragon is [testing].[14] Well, I can think of a few others dragons in the way, but testing is a good start.

14. Adapted from Russell, *Why I Am Not a Christian*, 47.

3

Credentialism

I'M A PRODUCT AND proponent of formal education, at least in part. I serve as an academic administrator and a professor of educational design and technology. I am also one of academia's strongest critics because I believe that we can do better, and can benefit society by reconsidering our role and resisting the temptation to hoard our power. As much as I treasure rich and vibrant academic communities, I also struggle with the way that our academic institutions wield power and control access and opportunity for people. We are gatekeepers, and while some can say that with pride, I write it with concern.

In 2014, I posted a suggested reading list on Twitter, "25 Must-Read Books for the Educational Hacktivist or Contrarian."[1] In reply, Charles Bingham, a education professor at Simon Fraser University, tweeted, "I appreciate your twitter focus on eduhacking. Thought you might like my TED talk."[2] Like myself, Bingham is a part of academia. He is a professor at a well-respected research institution, but he is also a critic who is deconstructing the modern building blocks of academia . . . at least to the extent that college becomes about earning credentials. For many, college is about more than that. It is also about community, connections, growing levels of competence and confidence, character formation, and creative expression. At least, that is what happens for

1. Bull, "25 Must-Read Books."
2. Quoted from Bull, "Credentials, Gatekeepers."

some amid their participation in higher education communities. For others, it is about getting . . .

> a piece of paper, so you can . . .

> get an interview, so you can . . .

> get a job that you like or want, so you can . . .

> get money, so you can . . .

I watched Bingham's TED Talk on "Why We Should Shred Our Diplomas," and so many of his ideas resonated with my own work and thought over the past couple of years, whether it be my investigation of credentialism, alternative education, unschooling, self-directed learning, personal learning networks, social entrepreneurship, or alternate credentials and open badges. The more I've come to study and understand the history and nature of academic credentials, the more I see that they are not the solution to our greatest social needs (nor are the educational institutions that offer them).

Good things happen in schools—plenty of good things. I'm just not convinced that the evolution of academic credentials to their current state is one of them. I write this as one who has four diplomas from higher education institutions, and who still finds himself drawn to pursuing two or three more. When I look at my diplomas (which is not often; they sit in a box in my office closet), it isn't hard for me to think that they mean that I'm somehow a little bit more special or valuable, but that isn't true. Nonetheless, they give me access that I didn't have before. They open doors to jobs and opportunities that never arose before getting that "terminal" degree. The title "Dr." breeds respect from no small number of people. I'm certain that I sometimes get the benefit of the doubt because of these credentials. I'm a little embarrassed about this, and the truth is that I've read, written, and studied fifty times more apart from my pursuit of those degrees. Most of what I write, say, and do comes from what I've learned through reading, doing independent research, networking, participating in various learning communities, experimenting, and trying things out in the real world. I learned things along the way toward getting those degrees that equipped me for doing these things, but I am certain that others could learn the same things without ever getting a single college diploma, let alone four.

In *Your Hidden Credentials*, Peter Smith used the example of the Scarecrow in *The Wizard of Oz* to illustrate the contemporary challenge with credentials. He explained that the Scarecrow did not need knowledge as much as he wanted recognition of what was already present. This is the situation with modern employers, as Smith explains:

> The Scarecrow thought he needed brains. But, what he really wanted was acknowledgement and recognition that he was a knowledgeable person with skills and learning that were valuable in the eyes of the world and to the people around him. The Wizard's recognition of what he knew gave the Scarecrow the confidence he had been lacking. With that recognition and the confidence it inspired, the Scarecrow was empowered.[3]

This is one of my struggles with how we've shaped modern education. We've made it exclusive. In many aspects of society, we've minimized the value of learning that is not credentialed. We've excluded the self-taught. We've allowed credential-bearing institutions to be gatekeepers for entry into no small number of professions or disciplines. What social good comes from this exclusive approach? Who are the winners? Who are the losers? Isn't it possible to imagine alternate models that are more open and welcoming of multiple routes toward competence?

In his TED Talk, Bingham says,

> South Africa was a very credentialed society. People had to carry what was called an apartheid passbook. In this passbook, it said your race. It said if you were an African, or an Indian, or a white person, or a colored person. And if, for example, you were an African person, a black person, and you decided to go into a whites only area after dark, a policeman could stop you and ask to see

3. Smith, *Your Hidden Credentials*, 15.

your apartheid passbook. If that passbook did not give
you the privilege to be in the white area after dark, then
you'd be put in jail.[4]

I'm convinced that these days we have our own version of the apartheid passbook (albeit with significantly different implications),
and it's called a diploma. These days it is not legal to discriminate
against a person based upon race. It is, however, perfectly legal
to discriminate against a person based upon educational attainment, based upon a diploma that a person does or doesn't have,
that was or was not received from this or that school. As Bingham
explained, ". . . And please don't take as many years as I did to realize that people don't need teachers like me."[5]

It may seem like too a strong statement to juxtapose South
African passbooks and academic credentials. Nonetheless, the
comparison invites us to consider whether modern academic credentials help or hinder our aspiration toward increased access and
opportunity for people. It challenges us to consider whether there
are alternatives that better respect learning, achievement, and
competence regardless of how it is acquired. It challenges us to ask
whether leaders in formal schooling value learning and intellec-
tual achievement enough to honor it wherever it is found, whether
it is present in the "credentialed" or the "uncredentialed."

Academic degrees and credentials are certainly not without
value. They can serve as symbols of achievement, even as indirect
evidence of competence. They speak to the hard work, commitment, and formal learning journey of a person as well. It is when
we mistake the credential for being inseparable from what it
represents that we run into more trouble. To have a credential is
not equal to being competent or a person of character. Most of society accepts these academic credentials as signs that you must
have certain traits and capabilities that make you worthy of certain
opportunities that are withheld from others. As such, we exclude
people from access to jobs and opportunities that would allow the
uncredentialed to make wonderful and positive contributions.

4. Bingham, "Why We Should Shred Our Diplomas," 10:47.
5. Ibid., 14:30.

Isn't it interesting that degrees don't have expiration dates or don't require ongoing demonstration of competence? Part of what draws me to startups and entrepreneurship is that credentials don't cut it. The startup community is a place where you can find high school dropouts mentoring PhDs, and graduates of unknown liberal arts colleges or state schools going head to head with Ivy League grads. And what they produce often trumps the prestige of their alma mater. Of course, there are startups, VC firms, and incubators that probably give more attention to a person with Stanford or MIT on the résumé, but the startup world is a place where they are not the only ticket to the show.

When I first got out of college, I became a middle school and high school teacher. I was so interested in whether people saw me as a good teacher. At some point, that was not enough. I wanted to actually be a good teacher, although having the respect of others was a nice thing to have too. I love the part of the startup world where people place so much more value on what you've done and what you can do than on your credentials.

Consider how some of the "best" students in classes get more passionate about getting an A than doing things of substance. Think about how we have a National Honor Society (NHS), and the baseline criterion has to do with grade point average (GPA). The students who are staying up late nights, devouring books, experimenting, exploring, and applying ideas they have learned, but doing so at the cost of an A, are not at the NHS banquets. They don't get celebrated in schools nearly as often as the people who focus their performance on earning the grades that lead to earning the credential. As such, many learning organizations celebrate credential earning more than deep learning.

This is why I've become an advocate for alternative credentials like open badges, certificates, and portfolios as a means of displaying competence. I hold out hope that they can provide alternatives (not necessarily replacements) for more traditional credentials. More routes reach more people. We add new academic currency that may not be well known or understood by most today, but still have the promise of lessening the stronghold of credentialing gatekeeper institutions. In doing so, they also open our eyes to possibilities for a more open and accessible way to recognize learning, competence, and achievement.

For decades, academic institutions serving "non-traditional" students gave opportunities to earn what is called "prior learning credit." It is a way of translating learning from life and work into college credit, allowing you to skip a few steps along the way to an academic credential. This plays an important role because academic institutions are still the credential gatekeepers in many areas. Yet, it is not difficult to imagine skipping the gatekeeper, devising open credentials that are used to recognize prior learning without the review of a traditional academic institution.

People already do this with their online presence. You can show your competence through your blog and/or digital portfolio, and even more broadly through your online activity. Candidly, I get enough consulting requests to replace or far exceed my university salary simply through contacts via my blog. If such a thing were increasingly common, this could be a game changer for how we think about credentials and different pathways to learning.

This is especially true in more emerging professions, ones that are not closely lined up with university majors or curricula. It is also the nature of some fields like programming or graphic design, especially when looking for consultants and contracted workers. If I want to hire people to develop a high-quality video, I don't care about their credentials; I want to see their portfolio and their references. Can they do great work? Can they meet a deadline and satisfy the needs of a client? Show me that they can do it well and for a reasonable price, and I am ready to hire them.

I'm less comfortable with that approach when it comes to picking a surgeon. I want assurance that I have a highly competent person, and I seem to trust that going through medical school and remaining board certified is good enough. Even then, I might also want to check patient reviews, get evidence that they stay current with emergence research and best practices, and make sure they don't have a long list of malpractice lawsuits lined up. For such professions, I understand the value of more carefully controlled pathways to the credentials. However, I an open to lessening the gatekeeping even in these professions as long as there is some sort of robust criteria for demonstrating competence. Besides, the number of professions that fit into such a category is relatively small.

The relationship between credentials and increased access and opportunity is a complicated one, and academic institutions offer a way to simplify things. The problem is that simplifying a complex problem may create other problems. The problems we've created are ones related to access and opportunity, to unnecessary exclusion of competent people, and to monopolized credentials. I don't expect things to change quickly. I'm not even sure if they will broadly change. Regardless, I see alternatives that seem to offer the promise of social good around openness, access, and opportunity; and I believe that we will see this demonstrated on the micro level as people experiment with and apply alternative credentials as a form of social/educational entrepreneurship.

Consider this proposal from David Labaree:

> In this book, however, I argue that it is time to consider whether the connection between schooling and social mobility is doing more hard than good. I show that the process of getting ahead often interferes with getting an education, and that the process of getting an education frequently makes it harder to get ahead. My aim is not to make the familiar—and generally valid—point that education grants its benefits disproportionately to those who are socially privileged. That argument naturally leads to the conclusion that we need to remake the educational system around a purer model of individual competitive achievement. My approach leads in quite a different direction. Instead of arguing that we need to make education into a more equitable mechanism for getting ahead, I argue that we need to back away from the whole idea that getting ahead should be the central goal of education.[6]

---

6. Labaree, *How to Succeed in School without Really Learning*, 1.

The Lincoln Test

In conclusion to this chapter, I offer a test for credentials in formal education. I call it the "Lincoln test." It is a simple test. Abraham Lincoln had less than two years of formal education and practiced law without earning a degree. He took the road less traveled to becoming both a lawyer and the President of the United States. The Lincoln test can be summarized in a few simple questions.

1. To what extent can someone have access to this through self-study and alternative pathways?

2. Does this career, group, association, or other entity leave room for modern learners who are the equivalent of Abraham Lincoln?

3. Is competence given a higher priority than credentials?

I like to think that the US government, for example, passes the Lincoln test. Even to this day it is possible for one to run and be elected or appointed to many posts in the government apart from holding formal credentials (with the exception of a US birth certificate or other credentials associated with citizenship). The same is true for starting a business and even practicing law in some parts of the country.

Still, many other parts of modern society quickly fail the Lincoln test. These are the ones that restrict access on the basis of specific credentials that often have prescribed pathways for learning. The Lincoln test allows us to challenge our assumptions about credentials, to beware of mistaking a symbol (diploma, certification, license) for actual competence to perform a job with quality. Abraham Lincoln certainly provides us with a historical example of one who was indeed competent without holding the standard credentials.

4

Non-Cognitive Skills

WHAT REALLY SETS PEOPLE up for well-being in life, as well as the ability to make significant contributions to their community, nation, and world? Is it a high GPA, high test scores, or high performance on other standardized tests aligned to the Common Core or some other set of academic standards? Content and academic disciplines are important, but our national conversation about education is suffering from an overemphasis upon standardized tests and an underemphasis upon what a growing body of literature indicates has a massive impact on the lives and opportunities for people. I'm talking about a set of traits sometimes called "non-cognitive skills."[1] Books like Paul Tough's *How Children Succeed* give us a glimpse into the power and importance of things like grit, curiosity, and character, but few schools make this, what I call, their "unavoidable, undeniable, school-shaping concept." Imagine what would happen if schools focused on nurturing grit, curiosity, and character as much or more than they are focused on aligning everything to the Common Core or striving to produce the highest standardized test scores. In this age of data and measurement, how many are even analyzing the data about how students are faring in these non-cognitive areas? If we are going to be an education

1. In sharing this term with other people, I find no shortage of confused looks and arguments that we need a better term. In fact, what some refer to as "non-cognitive skills" is also referred to as "character traits" or "signature strengths" by others. For more on this, see Kamentz, "Non-Academic Skills."

system focused on testing, why not at least make non-cognitive skills the primary measures?

Having a conversation with a colleague, I found myself thinking out loud about the role of assessment and grading in education. Many current grading practices are about rating and categorizing people. Even as I think about my own experiences in high school, I remember the special care administrators took with the straight-A students and those who had exemplary scores on their ACT or SAT. Those were identified as the exceptional students, the ones destined for great things. There is no question that high test scores and marks open doors to certain colleges that would otherwise be a long shot for students. We also see that test scores and GPA are indicators of one's likelihood to find academic success in college.[2] What about after college? That is where the research becomes more difficult. Earning a college degree increases the likelihood of certain opportunities after college, so having a greater likelihood of success in college naturally leads to greater opportunities after college, as indicated by a 2014 study.[3] On the flip side, there were also 2013 headlines about a Google human resource executive claiming that test scores and GPA were not especially helpful in finding the great talent they seek.[4] In addition, we have a growing collection of studies showing the importance of non-cognitive skills in the workplace, not to mention in the rest of one's life.

What if we looked at GPA and standardized test scores separately? What insights might we glean? Some studies suggest that we might be wise not to do so, as GPA tends to be a stronger predictor of college success than test scores.[5] While not certain, this may well indicate that it is not the aptitude of the person as much as many non-cognitive traits that make a difference. Grit, self-discipline, creative problem solving, interpersonal skills; these make a huge difference in the academic success of a person. If you

2. Hiss and Franks, "Defining Promise," 2.
3. Mientka, "High School GPA 'Strongly Predicts.'"
4. Soave, "Google Executive."
5. Belfied and Crosta. "Predicting Success in College," 13.

can't be disciplined enough to schedule time for in-depth study and preparation, your chances of academic success plummet, and since most of school is not "rocket science," it is less about your raw intelligence and more about discipline, hard work, and the emotional intelligence necessary to recover from temporary setbacks, to work hard, and to seek and obtain the help you need to be successful. Existing academic standardized tests don't measure such things.

This is coming from someone who is admittedly favorable to proposals for minimizing the role of letter grades and other proposals for creating space for more self-directed learning environments, but it is hard to deny that there are still plenty of people who find success in life having gone through traditional schools with letter grades, unit tests, desks lined up in straight rows, and a teacher lecturing at them from the front of the room. Yet it would be a mistake to assume that this validates all those methods directly. These schools are set up so students need to meet deadlines, learn to juggle multiple projects/subjects/assignments at once, schedule time to study and prepare for assignments, negotiate with leadership, learn from sometimes less than interesting or helpful lectures or lessons, stick to a routine, and do things that they don't want to do. Such demands can and do help some young people develop important non-cognitive skills.

My concern is that many such school contexts, while rewarding people who develop these skills (largely on their own or because of nurturing outside of school or in extracurricular activities), let many students fall between the cracks. This deflates and demoralizes some while affirming and empowering others. For example, I spoke with a colleague who teaches graduate students, and she noted a rise of schools returning to old educational practices that raise test scores (the growing priority in many public schools) while decreasing a broader range of skills and proficiencies that are not measured on such tests. Similarly, how many students go through school with the persistently reinforced implicit message that they are not smart, are bad at certain subjects, are a bad learner, and are not cut out for grand accomplishments? How many students have been deterred from reaching their highest potential by the current model?

As an alternative, what if learning organizations took as much interest in nurturing non-cognitive abilities like grit, leadership, managing emotions, building strong interpersonal relationships, and the like? The US Department of Education's mission statement is rooted in the concept of "global competitiveness."[6] Which nation is more competitive: a nation of people who meet the Common Core standards for math and language arts, or a nation of gritty, self-regulated, collaborative, emotionally and socially confident and competent people who boldly strive to accomplish great things in all aspects of life? Which will best position us to tackle many of our greatest challenges in our individual lives and in society as a whole? I'm not suggesting that math and language arts lack importance or that this needs to be an either/or debate. I am suggesting, however, that a nation of learning organizations focused on nurturing these non-cognitive skills will yield incredibly positive results in the lives of people, families, communities and beyond.

This is further supported by a 2015 study in which researchers looked at pro-social/emotional traits of kindergarten students, and how they did later in life. They found that these traits in young people correlated with positive outcomes in a wide variety of areas later in life. This included everything from education to work, mental health to substance abuse and their criminal record.[7] If we hope to nurture positive citizens and people who experience greater levels of health and well-being, then we are remiss to ignore the nurturing of non-cognitive skills in education.

Some schools and educators might argue that they do indeed teach non-cognitive skills. I don't challenge that claim. At the same time, it is hard to deny that test scores, standards, and GPA have center stage in contemporary American education. I'm fine with them playing a supporting role in this national drama, but I'd much rather see non-cognitive skills as the lead character. Of

6. US Department of Education, "Mission."

7. Jones et al., "Early Social-Emotional Functioning," para. 1.

course, this isn't new. Places like the KIPP (Knowledge in Power Program) schools are already deeply engaged in such an effort, even to the point of exploring a counterpart to the GPA known as the CPA (Character Point Average).[8] The idea of using a point system to measure character does not strike me as an especially promising or wise means of teaching and monitoring the development of character in young people, but their effort points to taking this aspect of growth seriously.

For a fascinating introduction to the broader range of non-cognitive skills, I encourage people to read an older text by Christopher Peterson and Martin Seligman called *Character Strengths and Virtues: A Handbook of Classification*. It is an impressive work that draws from a broad range of sources, from world religions to science.[9] As explained by the authors, it was intended to do the opposite of what is achieved with the *Diagnostic and Statistical Manual of Mental Disorders* (*DSM*), a text used widely by mental health professionals and researchers. Where the *DSM* focuses on disorders, *Character Strengths and Virtues* takes the positive psychology approach, looking at positive traits in individuals.[10] It provides an introduction to and explanation of what they refer to as character strengths and virtues, but this almost eight-hundred-page work then takes the reader through the current research and seminal authors on each of more than twenty traits, ranging from creativity and curiosity to humor and hope, love and kindness to citizenship and leadership, forgiveness and humility to prudence and self-regulation. It is an incredible resource for beginning to consider the possibilities of how we might create learning communities that celebrate, emphasize, and nurture such traits.[11]

8. Williams, "Science of Good Character," para. 2.

9. Peterson and Seligman, *Character Strengths and Virtues*, 33–52.

10. Ibid., 3–4.

11. At the time of publishing this book, *Character Strengths and Virtues* book is over a decade old. So much more research has been done on all of the traits discussed in this book since its publication. As such, I see this as a helpful launch pad for exploration, and not just a source text. I encourage people to use it as an introduction to the ideas, but then to expand one's study to the more current research on each topic. One simple way to start is to look at the

Critiques of Non-Cognitive Skills

This concept of teaching non-cognitive skills has its problems as well. As noted in an article by Jeffrey Snyder in the *New Republic*, there are at least three:

> The first is that we do not know how to teach character. The second is that character-based education is untethered from any conception of morality. And lastly, this mode of education drastically constricts the overall purpose of education.[12]

These critiques are clearly not insignificant. We have spent so little time focusing upon teaching character and non-cognitive skills that the well of knowledge about how to teach it is shallow. As such, if we can agree that this is an important part of one's education, then we must renew our interest in digging a much deeper well of knowledge and drawing from that. This will include new research, but also looking in other places for that knowledge.

While there might not be a massive body of empirical literature about how to teach character and non-cognitive skills, there are many traditions that have been far more committed to this for millennia. I realize that some readers will be resistant to this idea, but non-cognitive skills have always been highlighted in religious traditions, and while some might challenge such a claim, I find it hard to deny that the efforts in these traditions have been impactful. From an empirical standpoint, perhaps we can at least agree that sociocultural factors are critical in understanding how to nurture many non-cognitive skills.

As one who comes from a Lutheran Christian foundation, I am convinced that such a tradition has much to teach us about nurturing character and non-cognitive traits in people. Yet I don't think this needs to be a science-versus-religion debate. The two can support one another as we consider how to nurture these

---

scholars and sources cited, then researching to see what more current research they've completed. Of course, there are many new researchers not even quoted in the book, so a broader search is also warranted.

12. Snyder, "Teaching Kids 'Grit,'" para. 5.

important traits. As a way to illustrate this, I am going to draw from four distinct sources of insight. First, I will incorporate ideas introduced to me through my upbringing in a Christian context. Second, I will include insights from research about a concept known as deliberate practice. Third, I will draw from the Learning in Depth ideals popularized by Kieran Egan. Finally, I will add some insights that are popular among thinkers and proponents of project-based learning.

One example is James 1:2–4:

> Consider it pure joy, my brothers and sisters, whenever you face trials of many kinds, because you know that the testing of your faith produces perseverance. Let perseverance finish its work so that you may be mature and complete, not lacking anything.

It might seem like a simple concept, but this is a passage that parallels contemporary conversations about at least one part of the idea known as grit. This passage seems to indicate that persevering through difficulty is an important part of developing such a character trait. We don't need a massive body of literature to tell us that this is a valuable life skill, but the Bible passage tells us that working through challenging situations is partly how this develops.

Combine this with what we know from the empirical side, namely the research about deliberate practice that was popularized by what is now a classic on the subject by Anders Ericsson in 1993.[13] Ericsson explained that while practice is good, not all practice is equal. He pointed to something that he referred to as deliberate practice. It is not just about putting in the hours. It is about the right kind of practice, at least partly related to focusing your practices on developing areas of weakness. It is hard, focused, and not always pleasant, but one persists because it helps develop performance. There is a body of literature that can guide us in helping students learn to engage in deliberate practice to achieve their educational goals.[14]

13. Ericsson et al., "Role of Deliberate Practice."
14. While there is a growing body of literature in this area, for one of the

Let's add one more distinct line of thinking to this strand on perseverance and grit, drawing from some of the work by Kieran Egan. When I speak to audiences about project-based learning, the depth-versus-breadth conversation always comes up. I am usually the one to bring it up, but even if I don't, someone else will ask a question or make a comment related to it. Project-based learning provides individual students or small groups of students with an opportunity to spend an extended period of time digging deeply into a driving question or perhaps seeking solutions to a relevant problem or challenge. As a result, learners walk away from a successful project with deep knowledge about the topic at hand. Given all the time that the project takes, one criticism is that project-based learning sometimes results in learners missing out on a broad overview of a subject. In response, the project-based learning advocate might argue that the learner is developing skills that will last a lifetime, allowing one to learn many more things in the future. Another response might be to challenge the value of broad but shallow knowledge and question whether it will last. These sorts of conversations can go back and forth, with several valid points coming from both sides.

For some, the resolution to this debate comes by seeking to balance between project-based learning and other learning experiences that offer more breadth. One such example is not new, but I hear little mention of it in the United States. This is the Learning in Depth program,[15] championed by people like Kieran Egan (who is also known for being a critic of Dewey and the progressivism philosophy of education, as well as his work on imaginative education).

The Learning in Depth concept is simple. You keep a more traditional curriculum, but you add one significant element to it. In addition to all the other courses, you add a Learning in Depth course (although it may just be a few minutes a day) to the curriculum. The idea is that you randomly assign a simple topic to every learner, or, if you are starting with older students, you might

---

early and seminal works on the subject, see Ericsson et al., "Role of Deliberate Practice."

15. See the website at http://ierg.ca/LID/.

let them choose from a list. There are specific criteria for what constitutes a good topic. The topic might be something like dogs, light, sacred buildings, apples, or mountains. In some schools, this topic is assigned in the first grade and the student continues to study this topic for the next twelve years, developing an immense amount of knowledge, exploring it from dozens of angles. If your topic is cats, then you might study the biology of cats, learn about different types of cats, draw cats, take pictures of cats, study myths and legends about cats, look at environmental topics related to cats, and perhaps examine the role of cats in literature and film.[16]

There is little question that by the end of twelve years each student will have an area of expertise that exceeds almost everyone else they know. Advocates of this approach argue that it teaches research and inquiry skills, helps students discover the power of sticking with something for a longer period of time, builds confidence, helps students cultivate creativity and imagination, and that students learn any number of other skills along the way to becoming experts about their topic.[17]

What if we combine what we know from James 1:2–4, the research on deliberate practice, and the fascinating work around in-depth projects led by Kieran Egan? We start to see the possibilities for new types of learning environments that have great promise in nurturing any number of non-cognitive skills. How do you teach perseverance in a school context where the longest possible projects for many students only extends across a single semester? The deliberate practice research as well as the work around Learning in Depth both indicate that more time than that is necessary. This is certainly something that changes over time. There is much that students can and do learn from shorter learning experiences and projects, but some of these traits are also nurtured by longer and immersive experiences.

16. See Egan, *Learning in Depth*.

17. There are schools around the world that have adopted the Learning in Depth program, with fascinating stories about student learning. You can read some of these stories firsthand by following the links to participating schools on the Learning in Depth web site at http://ierg.ca/LID/.

While there might not be a deep well of knowledge about teaching character strengths, this does not make it a hopeless cause. We can look at learning communities where young people seem to be developing certain traits and take note of the context and environment in which they are nurtured. We can draw from diverse bodies of knowledge and pull them together for insights and getting informed about the possibilities. We can let go of our educational ruts that draw us back into the doing education in the same ways that we've done it before. We can invite young people into this conversation about the importance of such traits and collaborate with the students in exploring the research and how to develop such traits. By engaging in these activities, we can create learning contexts that are rich with learning content and developing character.

Non-Cognitive Skills amd Strength-Based Education

Should education be focused on deficiencies or strengths? While research that I've already mentioned in areas like deliberate practice points us to the value of focusing on our weaknesses, on a macro scale there is a compelling case for a strength-based approach, one that recognizes, celebrates, and invests in the unique strengths of each learner. Doing this requires reimagining what we do and how we do it in schools. Toward that end, consider the following eight principles of a strength-based approach to education that has promise in nurturing a growing sense of agency.

We can learn as much from studying people who are thriving as studying people who are struggling.

Strength-based education comes from the positive psychology movement. With early leaders like Martin Seligman, positive psychology decided to deviate from more traditional approaches to psychology that focused research on psychoses and neuroses, opting to spend more time studying positive traits. For example, it provides suggestions for treating depression, not only by studying people with depression, but also by studying people who have consistently positive emotions. Instead of only looking at Post-Traumatic Stress Disorder, it also looks for examples of post-traumatic growth. Or, we might learn about overcoming boredom and disengagement by studying the conditions under which people are highly engaged, or even in what Mihály Csíkszentmihályi referred to as "flow."[18] By learning from people at their best, we can identify lessons and principles that might help us and others experience such things as well.

We can help students learn and thrive by investing in their strengths as much as or more than addressing their deficiencies.

A deficiency approach to education focuses on discovering what students do not know or are bad at, and focusing the time and energy of students on remedying those deficiencies. A strength-based approach does not ignore deficiencies. We must address those deficiencies that are holding us back, but learners spend more time and energy on leveraging, refining, and expanding on their strengths. By doing so, the learners gain the self-confidence to grow in areas of deficiency eventually as well. This means that a strength-based approach to education places the emphasis upon what is going well with learners.

The goal of strength-based education is the equipping of confident, courageous lifelong learners, not just well-behaved, contributing citizens.

As noted by Lopez and Louis, "Strengths-based models embody a student-centered form of education with the primary goal of transforming students into confident, efficacious, lifelong learners whose work is infused with a sense of purpose."[19]

18. See Csikszentmihalyi, *Flow*.
19. Lopez and Louis, " Principles of Strengths-Based Education," 2.

41

Schools and educators measure what they value.

A strength-based approach not only measures student learning in traditional academic areas; it also seems to measure things like hope, well-being, positive character traits, leadership strengths, emotional intelligence, goal setting, creativity, engagement, and mindsets (as in Carolyn Dweck's growth mindset versus fixed mindset). Plenty of research indicates that these factors contribute to well-being and flourishing in life beyond school more than factual knowledge about content areas (not that those are to be ignored).

Strength-based education replaces one-size-fits-all learning with personalized learning.

If we change the goal of school to focusing upon helping students develop their strengths, that means different paths and destinations for different learners. It is for this reason that strength-based education usually provides students with opportunity to set some of their own goals, with teachers and others guiding them in their pursuit and achievement of those goals.

Strength-based education seeks to help students discover their unique combination of gifts, talents, and abilities to make a unique contribution to a world of "neighbors."

For those of you who watched Mr. Rogers as a kid, he often reminded viewers that they are unique and offer something that no one else in the world is capable of providing. I come from a Lutheran Christian background, so I frame this in terms of vocation or calling. What are my unique gifts, talents, and abilities, and how can I use them to love my neighbor? What would it look like if this were a driving question for all learners throughout their schooling?

Strength-based education nurtures an appreciation for the gifts, talents, and abilities of others.

If school is reframed as being about each learner developing his or her strengths, then it also provides wonderful opportunities to recognize, appreciate, and encourage the strengths in other learners, fostering a positive and mutually encouraging environment. As Proverbs 27:17 says, "As iron sharpens iron, so one person sharpens another."

8. Strength-based education helps students set, pursue, and achieve goals.

It helps students learn how to set goals, how to devise plans to achieve them, learn how to experiment with strategies and heuristics for pursuing goals, and learn how to learn. This is the spirit of the "teach a man to fish" approach to life.

What would it look like if our schools embraced these eight concepts? What would need to change? What would need to stay the same? How might it impact the present and future well-being of students? This offers us a means of thinking about schools that truly nurture non-cognitive skills, traits that promise important benefits for the individual who embodies them, not to mention the communities in which they live.

5

Agency

When I lead workshops, I sometimes like to start with a simple group icebreaker called Either/Or. I put a single statement on the screen: "Good teachers become less important." Then I invite the people in the room to stand up and represent their agreement or disagreement with the statement by their position in the room. "If you strongly agree with the statement, go to the right side of the room. If you strongly disagree with the statement, go to the left side of the room. If you are somewhere between those two extremes, take a position in the room that represents your stance." Then I invite teachers to explain their positions. At any time, teachers are welcome to change their position in the room based upon the insights shared by their colleagues.

As you might expect, this gets a room full of teachers talking. There are always people who represent both extremes, and there are plenty who end up somewhere in the middle. Those on the right side of the room defend the role of the teacher as a key guide, an expert, a mentor, and the coordinator of the learning experiences. The people on the left recognize those important roles but tend to argue that it is the teacher's job to help students develop a growing level of independence, to become less and less dependent upon the teacher as each student grows in competence, confidence, and a sense of agency.

This latter point is the reason for this chapter. Without any intent to devalue the role of a teacher, part of our goal in education should be to equip students for the capacity to learn independent of a teacher, to develop a sense of agency for both life and learning. As John Taylor Gatto argues, "Children allowed to take responsibility and given a serious part in the larger world are always superior to those merely permitted to play and be passive."[1] I am referring to the critical contemporary issue of human agency, the capacity to make choices for oneself, take ownership, and wield influence on oneself and one's environment. If our schools are focused on nothing more than nurturing compliance, then this is not necessary. If we need a society of people who take ownership and initiative, who have a growing sense of responsibility for themselves, then agency is indeed a critical issue in education.

As a way to illustrate the change that we want to promote in our learning organizations, I contrast a fish distribution center and a father teaching his son to fish. The first is a place where people can go to buy or receive fish that were caught and cleaned by others. It is easier and requires less of the recipient. Fishing lessons are qualitatively different. The father nurtures the boy, teaches him the details and skills needed to fish, and eventually the boy can catch, clean, and eat as many fish as he wants. He can even pass this skill to others. Applied to schools, the first model leaves the students persistently dependent upon others to teach them. The second seeks to help each learner become self-directed, a self-teacher, self-regulated, and a self-learner. This is the type of change and innovation that we want to promote in our schools. Traditional teacher-directed models risk failing to meet such a goal. What would it take for our school to shift from a fish distribution center to a place of fishing lessons? What would that look like?

On a personal note, my education expanded when I discovered that teachers were not at the center of learning, that they were not even essential in some cases. It took off when I recognized that the only essential elements of a learning experience are a learner and an experience. I am a teacher, so I must not take this line of thinking too literally, right? Oddly enough, I do take this literally, while continuing to believe that teachers play a very important

1. Gatto, *Underground History of American Education*, xv.

role in education and learning throughout life. It is just that I am a champion for a relationship between teacher and learning that nurtures a growing student of independence and agency, recognizing that this will be different for individual learners and that there are many ways to accomplish this.

I continue to believe that teachers have a valuable role in guiding and mentoring learners at different stages of their life and learning journeys. These people sometimes hold an official title of teacher or professor, or they might be a neighbor, friend, family member, or even a stranger. In one sense, a teacher is anyone or anything that contributes to our learning. With that definition, even your dog or pet rock can be a teacher.

This doesn't diminish a professional educator's role and impact, but it points to a truth that is perhaps more easily recognized in healthcare. Imagine an oncologist who, instead of nurturing a person back to health and the point of not needing further treatment or appointments, manipulates things so that the patient never quite reaches full health and has to return for treatment indefinitely. There are instances in healthcare where indefinite care is necessary for a person's condition, and I am open to the fact that this may be the case in education as well. Yet, even in these cases, there is the question about power and influence. Who is ultimately in control? In healthcare and education, choice and partnership with the patient or learner is an important aspect of keeping a person's agency intact.

When I think about the role of what we traditionally call a teacher, one goal of good teachers is to work hard at making themselves as unnecessary as possible—not unimportant in the sense of lacking value, but unnecessary in the sense that they are eventually no longer needed. In other words, the goal of the teacher is to aid the learners in becoming self-directed learners. Few disagree with this at some level. Our disagreement resides with the scope and timing. Where some of us differ is with regard to how soon we think the teacher should begin to step back and let the learner take control. Whatever the case, I continue to reflect upon the critical need to help students of all ages grow as self-determined and self-directed learners.

Good Teachers Become Less Important

Several years ago I wrote what became one of my most read blog posts, entitled "Good Teachers Become Less Important," part of which was incorporated into this chapter. I was delighted to see the rich conversation surrounding the article on LinkedIn groups, Twitter, and through a number of private messages and emails with readers. There is no question that I created the title to provoke thought and discussion. What I enjoyed about the title of the article is that it can be read in different ways, even though the article itself clarified the way that I was using it. If people read the title and did not go on to read the entire article, they might think I was claiming that teachers are somehow becoming less important or valuable. The title could be read as a sort of news headline, claiming that something has changed and good teachers suddenly have become less important. While it is true that the Internet and a variety of tools and resources are making it increasingly possible for us to learn apart from the traditional teacher and classroom environment, that was not my intended meaning in the title.

The title can also be read in a very different sense, as a sort of philosophy statement about something that I consider important in education. From that perspective, the title was drawing our attention to a fact that is largely intuitive, but is sometimes forgotten to the detriment of learners. Teachers have the role and responsibility of helping students move toward independence with regard to a variety of tasks. Good teachers learn to become increasingly less necessary as their students progress toward mastery of certain tasks. Imagine a math teacher whose students are no more capable of solving math problems on their own at the end of the year than they were at the beginning of the year. The math teacher might feel good about being needed by the students to solve the math problems, but that is not her job. Her job is to help students in such a way that they will be able to use math for the rest of their lives, to use it in situations where a math teacher is not present to help them. In other words, their job is to become less important, less necessary in the mathematical lives of the students. We can disagree about the best way to help students achieve such independence, but not as much about the goal of helping students become increasingly independent. This is too central and critical to a philosophy of education in a democratic society.

I noticed that one response to my first article described the teacher-student relationship as similar to that of a conductor and an orchestra. That can be a helpful comparison for describing the present interactions in some classrooms, but I don't think that it necessarily helps us think about the goals (future tense) of a good teacher, and this is part of my concern with too much of a teacher-centered approach to education. A teacher-centered approach risks focusing largely on the present behaviors and actions of the teacher in orchestrating a harmonious class session or a well-behaved student in the present.

Ultimately, the goal of education is not to provide a present and harmonious learning environment. Teaching has one foot in the present and one in the future, thinking about how students are progressing toward independence, self-regulation, and self-direction in a wide array of subjects and tasks. When students learn to drive, they usually have a guardian, guide, or driver's education instructor with them—but not forever. That guide becomes increasingly less important as the student learns to drive alone. If this doesn't happen, then little learning (and therefore little good teaching) has taken place. As a result, I contend that learning environments should help people develop at least a small measure of self-direction and self-regulation.

Some might argue that not all students are capable of independence and self-direction. Even if this were true, there is little question that almost all people can learn to be a bit more independent and self-directed than where they started. Part of good teaching involves helping to foster the types of spaces, experiences, and environments where students are able to develop this independence. Some learning environments are shaped more by the desire to keep students under control, ensure that they are coloring between the lines, and get them to follow the teacher's instructions. There are times to color between the lines and it is important to learn how to follow instructions, but it is also important to learn how to carry out tasks without instructions, to take the road less traveled, to learn through experimentation and exploration, and to take personal initiative.

Part of good learning involves engaging in activities and experiences that help us to progress toward self-direction and independence, learning more about how to leverage one's personal strengths, setting goals and establishing a plan to meet those goals. If teachers always set the goals and establish the plans, how are students supposed to learn these important skills? If teachers always establish the priorities, how do students learn to prioritize? This is why it is critical (for the sake of students and their learning) that good teachers learn to gradually (or sometimes rapidly, depending upon the learner and context) become less important, less directive, and less essential to the learning experience.

"But my students would do nothing if I didn't tell them what to do." That may be true, and I'm not arguing that teachers should never give instructions or direction. In many learning contexts, simply abandoning such actions would be negligence. However, here is the important question that good, even great, teachers use to inform their actions: "How I can help this student progress toward independence, toward functioning on a given task without my help, direction, or redirection?" Persistently asking and seeking answers to this question is an important step in helping to cultivating creative, courageous citizens and not simply compliant and submissive students.

Voice and Choice

Part of the agency discussion is related to the idea of giving students voice and choice in education. What are our biases and assumptions about student voice? What happens when we move from education as something done to students to something that students do themselves, or at minimum, that students are invested and involved in the decisions as much as we might expect of a major shareholders? What amazing visions for education could we make a reality if we tapped into the perspectives and brilliance of young people in our K–12 and higher education institutions?

Ask a group of educators how to solve a problem and, more often than not, we will suggest some sort of educational solution. We are wired that way. Ask a sociologist, psychologist, or theologian about a social problem and there is a good chance that they will do the same thing. They will look at it from their distinct lens and provide a sociological, psychological, or theological assessment, drawing from solutions most common in their fields. What does this mean for how we aspire to find solutions to education's greatest challenges today?

Interestingly, there are voices that are often muffled in education. More often than not, these voices are not involved in hiring decisions, the exploration of new possibilities, plans for quality improvement, innovations in teaching, learning, and curriculum, along with broader aspirations to address the digital divide, access and opportunity, workforce development, and more. We rarely involve the students.

In 1995, Kathryn Church wrote a groundbreaking book about mental health called *Forbidden Narratives: Critical Autobiography as Social Science.* Unlike many other books about mental health, this text included the author's own lived experiences, finding herself in the curious position of being both a mental health professional and a mental health patient. Reading this lived experience of a researcher and patient changed the trajectory of my work and research. I was introduced to the important world of auto-ethnography and autobiography as research.

This research method continues to be challenged by more than a few in the social sciences, but it opened my eyes to the fact that much research fails to take us deeply into the lived experiences of people from their own perspectives.[2] Researchers, as much as we try, paint the picture of others' lived experiences, but

2. Holt, "Representation, Legitimation, and Autoethnography."

we hold the paintbrush. Apart from select excerpts that illustrate a theme or concept, the subjects do not have opportunity to let their voices be directly heard. It is a controlled and systematic reporting of the findings from the researcher's viewpoint, but it does not necessarily represent the nuance and voice of each subject in the study. Some researchers are better at this than others, but they rarely achieve what can be experienced when we hear directly from the subjects.

Applying this lesson from Church's work, I contend that we have the same challenge as we pursue opportunities and innovations in education. We survey students. We might run focus groups. We observe and analyze student motivation, engagement, persistence, learning, and more. Far less often do we invite the students into the designing of schools, curricula, and courses. How often do they help shape what, how, when or where they learn? How do we engage them in prioritizing, budgeting, establishing policy and practice?

Some argue that it is wise not to engage the learners in such important work, that it is best left to the expert educationists or academic professionals. Yet, look at higher education institutions around the world and academics are making educational decisions when they often have little to no formal training in the field of education. Policy makers are making important decisions that shape the future of education when many have done little to read, research, and study deeply in the areas that they are influencing. Even those trained in education are consistently making education decisions based on their personal experience or preferences as much or more than their study of the research or by tapping into a solid body of evidence-based practice. Given these realities, why would it be out of line to empower students to own not only their learning but also the communities in which they learn?

Student voice is also important because we are trying to nurture a generation of people who have a voice and use it in the world. We want active citizens and participants in communities. If we want to nurture a generation of compliant consumers who just do what they are told by authorities, then not giving voice is a great plan. If we want them to help shape their communities, then we need to help them learn how to own and participate in a community that they can influence in positive ways.

The Good News

The good news is that this is happening, even if just in small ways. When I visited Western Sydney University in 2015, I saw this beautiful university library rich with collaborative spaces, study spaces, «silent» spaces, and even a sleep pod for those students needing a quick nap between a day of work and evening classes. When I asked about the design decisions, I learned that the students had an active say in much of it. In fact, there is a portion of the annual library budget that the students control, allowing them to pursue ongoing innovations.

In classrooms and schools around the country, school leaders and teachers are inviting students to establish and shape everything from classroom rules to what and how they will learn. This is especially true in many schools embracing the self-directed learning movement making its way around the world. I've had the joy and honor of witnessing this firsthand at places like Acton Academy in Austin, Texas, KM Global in Wales, Wisconsin, and Amazing Grace Christian School in Seattle, Washington. In fact, learning about the original formation of KM Global, a project-based and personalized learning charter school with a global focus, Dr. Valerie Schmitz explained that no small measure of the original vision for the school came from a team of students that she consulted.

How to Involve Students

How does a learning organization get serious about this? For those educators who are reading this, how do they get started? Here are some possibilities to consider.

1. Create a team of students who help make decisions about the physical spaces in the learning organization.

2. Have a combined team of students, teachers, and other related stakeholders to meet 4+ times a year to plan key curricular innovations, including school-wide projects and timely elements of the curriculum.

3. Involve student voices in the interview process of new employees, ranging from administrators and janitorial staff to teachers and coaches.

4. For secondary and higher education especially, create a student advisory committee for each department/college/school.

5. Create a means of obtaining formal feedback about the school culture, curriculum, and experience at least once a week.

6. Encourage teachers to establish small teams of students that work with the teacher to design, revise, and adjust lessons and units as the school year progresses.

7. In formal and intentional ways, invite and create specific ways for students to become growing experts on teaching and learning research and practice.

8. When new projects, innovations, practices, models and resources are being considered, have teams of students play an active role in the research, review, and decision. In fact, why not have means by which students can propose and initiate such things?

Student voice matters in education today. Listening to those voices and, even more, entrusting students with decisions about the nature of their learning communities has tremendous benefits. I am not just referring to future benefits in terms of test scores and measurable academic gains. I am also looking at the benefits of creating more equitable and humane learning communities for today. We see this happening in promising ways, but what if we saw it even more? What if we found ways to persistently engage students in tackling some of education's greatest challenges and pursuing some of its greatest opportunities? What if the students had more room to imagine the possibilities and to pursue them?

6

Purpose and Meaning

IT IS HARD TO get motivated without a sense of purpose or meaning. Ask any teacher about one of the more common complaints of
students in school and they will tell you that it is a question of relevance. "Why are we learning this? What is the purpose of studying this?" Without an answer to questions of relevance, purpose,
and meaning, it is difficult to stay engaged. Again, this is where
our contemporary education reform focus on topics like standards
and testing falls short. These efforts lack a compelling reason that
resonates with learners.

In my book *Missional Moonshots: Insights and Inspiration for
Educational Innovation*, I recalled a story from one of the profes-
sors in my graduate study years ago. He told us about a researcher
who decided to explore the question of why students fall asleep in
class.

> When I was in graduate school years ago, one of my pro-
> fessors told the story of a doctoral student who chose to
> study the reasons why students fall asleep in class, using a
> qualitative research method known as grounded theory.
> In that method, you start with a core research question
> and then conduct in-depth interviews with the popula-
> tion of people who are most likely to help you answer
> that research question.
>
> The researcher interviewed students who fell asleep
> in at least one class during the past semester. As he con-
> ducted the interviews, he began to develop a theory that

provided an answer to his core research question. Then he interviewed more people, seeing if data from those subsequent interviews supported or deviated from his existing theory. He adjusted his theory to accommodate the data from each new interview, continuing this process until he had a theory that adequately explained the data gathered from all of the interviewees.

Finally, the researcher distilled his theory about why students fall asleep in class down to a simple two-word phrase, "perceived meaninglessness." In other words, the reason students fell asleep in class had nothing to do with how the students felt, how much they had slept the night before, or any other such physical explanation. When learners perceive that what is happening in a class lacks meaning, they lose motivation and are more likely to fall asleep.[1]

We can invest countless dollars into adding the latest technology in our schools and classrooms, curriculum design and development, teacher professional development, aligning with new standards, and countless other items. But unless we take seriously questions and issues related to meaning and purpose, we are likely to fall short in our education reform efforts. Meaning matters.

It matters for individual students, and it also matters for the schools themselves. I've worked with many K–12 schools, universities, startups, and non-profit organizations on projects related to educational innovation or educational technology. I've visited, observed, and interviewed leaders in countless other organizations. After all of that consulting and learning, I'm convinced that one of the most significant differences between the organizations and innovations that thrived and those that struggled came down to meaning, purpose, and vision. Those that thrived had vision for what they wanted to accomplish and it was informed by a deep-seated sense of purpose or meaning. The high-impact educational innovations were not just about being innovative or trendy. The leaders had a clear and compelling vision for why they were pursuing something new. They had a noble cause. They had something

1. Bull, *Missional Moonshots*, 8.

that would inspire them to get out of bed in the morning and be excited or at least committed to devote another day to something of substance.

When Victor Frankl wrote *Man's Search for Meaning* in the 1940s, recounting the lives and struggles on those in Nazi concentration camps, he discovered something important about the role of meaning and purpose on a person's life. He saw firsthand the power of a *why* to keep someone going in even the most grim of circumstances.

> Nietzsche's words, "He who has a why to live for can bear with almost any how," could be the guiding motto for all psychotherapeutic and psychohygienic efforts regarding prisoners. Whenever there was an opportunity for it, one had to give them a why—an aim—for their lives, in order to strengthen them to bear the terrible how of their existence. Woe to him who saw no more sense in his life, no aim, no purpose, and therefore no point in carrying on. He was soon lost.[2]

If a why can do that for a person enduring life in a concentration camp, how much more can it shape, animate and inspire learners and learning organizations? This means that an impactful educational effort must move beyond common answers. When a learner asks why about what they are learning, this is an opportunity, not a challenge. "We do it because I said so." "We do it because that is what the state requires." "We do it because this is how we've always done it." "It was good enough for people in the past, so it is good enough for us." None of these answers provide a deep sense of meaning and purpose in the work. None of them offer a compelling reason. If we want learners to be deeply invested and engaged in their work, we are wise to help them discover a why that matters for them. If we want our learning organizations to thrive, we are wise to not just help them write a mission or vision statement, but to find one that they are proud to live and that truly shapes everything that they choose and do in the organization.

2. Frankl, *Man's Search for Meaning*, 84.

Learning from Innovative Learning Organizations

A number of years ago I committed to visiting innovative learning organizations. I retell this work in greater detail in my book on *Missional Moonshots*, but I will share only a fraction of that work here in order to point out the importance of meaning and purpose. I wanted to learn from these innovative organizations, but I was especially interested in seeing if there were consistent traits among the leaders and others in these organizations. I observed, interviewed, and studied primary documents, and there is so much that I learned.

As I visited countless independent schools and charter schools, I was consistently amazed by the distinct cultures in these schools. Many of these were places where the students felt safe and were engaged. They took ownership in the learning community. The same was true about the leaders and the teachers. In fact, one of the things that was hard to miss was how much the schools leaders and teachers were on the same page about the mission, vision, values, and goals of the schools. Unlike some schools where certain teachers close their doors and just do their own thing, these were schools where the mission dripped from every practice, policy, and activity in the school. There was a unity in mission and purpose among those who worked in these schools, and that spread to the students as well.

When I interviewed leaders of these schools, many of them were the founders. They had been involved in creating the vision for the school and brining it to life. As such, they had a huge stake in the institution's success. Even more, no small number of these leaders has a vision that was inspired by a personally meaningful experience. It might have been someone who led or taught in a traditional school and was disenfranchised by the system to the point that they were ready and willing to pursue the road less traveled. Some of the founding leaders were parents inspired to create a school that they dreamed of having for their own children—one that was less about compliance, politics, and lifeless policies, and more about students, their learning, their well-being, their engagement, and their sense of learning and calling in life.

Interestingly, I studied a broad range of schools. I researched self-directed learning academies, project-based learning schools, core knowledge schools, leadership academies, classical schools, faith-based schools, and many others. While these had nearly opposing visions and missions, what they had in common was how seriously they took their missions. They protected them by being relentless in their review of candidates to teach or work in the organization. They sifted anything and everything through that mission before it became part of the school.

In doing this hard work, they succeeded in creating school communities and cultures with a strong sense of meaning and purpose. Their distinctives didn't draw or resonate with every prospective student or family, but for those who opted to go to the school these were schools that typically garnered high ratings and praise from the students and the parents. The students and parents knew what the schools was about and where it stood on important issues, and they had a choice about whether to be at the school

This is in stark contrast to other schools that struggle to have a cohesive vision, mission, set of values, or purpose that is upheld and pursued by every employee in the organization. These more typical schools too often have mixed messages, competing missions, people with hidden agendas, and too many political pressures that find their way into the classrooms and design of the learning communities. How could we expect meaning and purpose to be evident in such a context?

I've visited enough schools to believe that the foundation to great schools is a clear and compelling mission, vision, or some other statement that gives them a clear sense of purpose. While pretty much every school on the planet has such statements in a formal document, that doesn't mean that they are alive or compelling. Some mission statements, for example, are so long and packed with buzzwords that people struggle to understand them or rally behind them. Others are so generic that they fail to inspire. Others are so tactical that they talk significantly about the how but don't give anyone a compelling why or reason for the organization existing.

With that said, I've found little evidence to suggest that the terminology, length, or any other syntax issue matters as much as finding something that gives direction and inspires, and is then used persistently and relentlessly by everyone in the community. It is a description of the culture and community that they not only aspire to become, but that they are committed to embracing and protecting.

As I've already stated in this chapter, meaning matters. It matters for individual students. They need to see meaning in what they are learning. They need to know and have opportunity to explore the why behind the what of learning. They further benefit from and thrive most when they have opportunity to be in a learning community where the school leaders, teachers, parents, and others are of one voice on the core elements of who they are, what they are, and why they are. When this is present, we have the foundation upon which to build some of the most impactful learning organizations in the world.

There is no reason why we can't pursue this for every learning organization on every level. There are certainly political barriers and external pressures that make this difficult, but not impossible. When you find an organization with this type of focus, it is a force with which to be reckoned. You might be surprised by the impact that it can have, near and far.

In fact, many such organizations around the country are so substantive that their ideas spread. Acton Academy started with a single school in Austin, Texas, but it is know spreading throughout the United States and beyond. The same is true for many other distinctive schools with a clear purpose. We see it with KIPP schools, core knowledge schools, project-based learning schools, and Agile Learning Centers. We are bound to see many more such schools on the K–12 level emerge in the upcoming years, and it is likely to spread to the university level in interesting ways in the future as well.

I am so confident because we are in a time where people crave meaning, purpose, and distinctiveness. As much as there are pressures for test scores, high GPAs, and other such modern educational trappings, people still want something meaningful. This is likely why choice programs and charter schools continue to flourish. It is also why many university advertisements and marketing campaigns gravitate toward messages about purpose, calling, and mission. Now all we need is for more learning organizations to take these missions and purposes so seriously that they are willing to sift everything that they are and do through it.

7

The Digital Divide

I DEDICATE THIS CHAPTER to everyone who has heard or read the term "digital divide" but didn't know what others were talking about. Or, perhaps you have a general idea, but you wouldn't be in a position to have an informed conversation about it. It is a term that people hear on occasion, but few people with whom I speak are actually sure what we mean by it, or whether it is an important issue. I contend that it is an important issue, but in a different sense than how many others write and think about it.

How would you feel about taking a cross-country trip without a cell phone? Over the past decade I have conducted informal surveys during presentations to various groups. I ask them about their comfort level traveling cross-country without a cell phone. While it is just an informal experiment, there is a clear trend. In general (yes there are certainly exceptions), the younger the person, the more anxiety he or she seems to have about the idea of a disconnected road trip. Maybe it is because more young people have never known life without a cell phone, or perhaps it is something else. Whatever the case, the cell phone is a technology that has transformed the way that we think about communication. I'm certain that it is changing values, highlighting the value of being continually connected to select friends and family, regardless of physical location. And yet, this connectivity is not everywhere. There continue to be people all around us who have limited access to computers, cell phones, the Internet, and other current technologies. Or they may have access but lack the necessary confidence, knowledge, or skills to make use of these technologies.

It may be due to a financial issue, or because they live in an area with limited access. They may live in a place where there is ample technology, but firm restrictions limit access to large portions of the Web. For others, it is a self-restriction due to a fear of technology or a lack of interest in learning how to use the new tools. Some call this the digital divide. Those who are concerned about this issue argue that limited access prevents people from full participation in society, as well as decreased economic and educational opportunity. It even limits their ability to cultivate critical contemporary communication skills that have a direct impact upon one's success in both work and school. Consider something simple like finding and applying for a new job. If you don't have access to the Internet and knowledge of how to find job databases and use them, then you are at a huge disadvantage in the workforce today. The same is true with more complex tasks in the digital world.

Digital Divide Causes

There are at least six distinct digital divide causes, each with their own limitations and potential solutions. As you will see from this list, we are nearing ubiquitous access to the Internet, but that does not guarantee a solution to many of the causes. This is not just technological. It is sociological, psychological, even political as well.

Self Restrictions

This is present in people who are afraid of or who are intentionally avoiding technology. As a result, they find themselves cut off from society or at a disadvantage in certain situations. We might not see this as common issue among the youngest people in society, but it is a challenge with older members of society. I continue to see it among some educators. As such, they develop an attitude about technology that could significantly harm their employment opportunities in the near future. As many people often say today, technology is unlikely to replace teachers in the near future, but teachers with technology may soon replace teachers without it. In addition, if a teacher's fear limits his use of technology in positive ways, this also decreases valuable learning opportunities for the students being served by that teacher.

Low Access

These are is typically people in communities with limited access due to poverty or limited resources (both urban and rural communities). We are well on our way toward ubiquitous access to the Internet, and the cost of devices continues to decrease. However, we are not there yet, and this continues to be an important issue. Even if schools are well connected, students in homes without connections do not have ongoing access, putting them at a disadvantage when it comes to doing research and using the Web as a tool for enhancing and supplementing what happens during regular school hours.

Limited Training

This refers to people in schools that do not provide adequate training. We are far beyond the days of a basic typing or computer skills class in high school as adequate. Today more people are considering the value of computer programming as a more standard offering in schools. In addition, while many schools have embraced topics like digital literacy, we persist in problems when it comes to deep information literacy and research skills on the web, learning how to build a robust personal learning network, or having a deep dive look at the world of programming that is shaping and reshaping our world.

Some schools still do not even offer computer programming, or if they do, it is an elective for a few technology-minded young people. Coding is not just preparation for computer science jobs. It is an introduction to the syntax that animates the digital world and integrates with almost every aspect of our lives. As such, some argue that this is an important part of being educated in a digital age.

We live in an increasingly programmed world. Our cars, computers, phones, television, healthcare, movies, music, and education are all influenced by programming languages. Yet, many of us don't read or write in a single programming language. We can certainly have thoughts and opinions about each of these areas, but understanding what goes on beneath the hood might help with those thoughts. Of course, there is the added benefit of being able to program parts of the world around us. As Dan Crow wrote, "Software is the language of our world."[1] So, why not learn about this language?

Consider the following nine benefits of learning to program.

1. It helps teach logic, systematic and analytical thinking.

2. As a result, it is excellent training for developing problem-solving skills.

3. It gives us insight into the programmed world around us.

4. It gives us a useful skill in today's world.

5. We can write our own programs.

6. Of course, unless you devote significant time, there will be far better programmers out there, the people you want to write some of the most important programs in your work on life. And yet, learning to program will help you learn how to communicate more effectively with those programmers.

7. It opens doors to new career opportunities or might enhance current careers (sometimes in unexpected ways).

---

1. Crow, "Why Every Child Should Learn to Code."

8. It is rewarding and confidence-building to create something with your ideas, even if it isn't a masterpiece or the foundation of the next Microsoft.

9. It might give you insights on how software works, the software you use each day.

For these and other reasons, this issue even captured the attention of the President of the United States. In President Obama's 2016 State of the Union address, he argued for the importance of "offering every student the hands-on computer science and math classes that make them job-ready on day one."[2] And in a 2013 video Obama said, "Learning these skills isn't just important for your future. It's important for our country's future."[3] This aligns closely with the stated mission of the US Department of Education, which includes "preparation for global competitiveness." There is no question that computer science continues to play an increasingly large role in the workplace and society.

Adding more opportunities in formal schooling make sense as well, but what about making computer science something as ubiquitous as math or some other "core" course? Should legacy high schools start adding computer science or programming as a graduation requirement? Should it become a new part of the core offering for K–12 students? Proponents argue that this is a critical twenty-first-century skill. Others argue that, even though not everyone will use the knowledge, it is a good way to find top talent and direct them toward those careers.

Lack of Immersion

As I mentioned before, people who have the technology and access in their schools and public community spaces but not at home may still be at a disadvantage. As such, they are more likely to be literate, but not fluent; they speak technology with a strong accent.

2. Obama, State of the Union, para. 21.
3. Obama, "President Obama Asks," 0:16.

This lack of fluency puts them at a slight or significant disadvantage depending upon the situation.

We know that the quality of one's formative years of learning is not just about the quality of one's schooling. It is a broader ecosystem of learning that matters for people. This includes the home environment, access to rich community and cultural experiences, involvement in extracurricular activities, and others. Interview many people in science and technology fields, for example, and you will find that their hobbies and activities outside of schools had a significant influence on their future career paths. People who made extraordinary contributions in their fields or reached grand achievements are often characterized by what they did outside of the classroom as much or more than what they did in the classroom.

This is because excellence calls for immersion, countless hours of practice, exploration, and experimentation. This is an advantage in the connected world as well. Where are the times and contexts when young people get a chance for unstructured experimentation or getting lost in a project of personal interest? The education system in a connected world is much larger than what happens in school.

Restricted Access

While the outcomes might be similar to the last category, I find it necessary to at least provide a distinct cause focused upon people in locations that have high levels of censorship. They might have access to many things, but their ability to learn from diverse viewpoints is censored or restricted. This might come from a national policy or practice in some countries around the world, but it also happens in some schools with strict regulations and software that locks down anything dangerous or controversial.

Such software is commonplace in schools within the United States, and people make a compelling case for protecting young people from accidentally venturing onto a dangerous or "inappropriate" website. At the same time, there is a counter to this position that argues for opening up access as students develop, helping them to navigate these digital streets for themselves and learn to regulate. This is a different issue, but I include it here because it sometimes impacts a person's ability to learn how to navigate the "real digital world."

Unlimited Access

This refers to people who have ample access and no restrictions or guidance. This is an unusual one, but one that is getting more attention. They have the access, but have not learned how to self-monitor, how to unplug, and how to analyze the affordances and limitations, the benefits and the dangers. They often suffer from over-media-cation and miss out on life beyond the screen. I will devote more attention to this one in a forthcoming chapter.

The Digital Divide and the Connected World

The idea of the digital divide evolved over time. In the 1980s through the early 2000s, there was still reference to those who do and those who do not have access to hardware or the Internet. Then the focus shifted to those who know how to use it and those who do not know how to use it. In other words, there has been a shift from a lack of physical access to a lack of knowledge, skill, and ability in using what is available to us. You can give two people the exact same set of tools and see completely different results based upon their knowledge and skill with those tools. Give me a world-class violin and you will not see the same result as you would if you gave it to a trained violinist.

This is where we are in the digital divide. It is less about the technology itself, although that is still an important issue that should not be overlooked in other parts of the world. It is now about finding ways to nurture growing competence, confidence, even expertise in taking advantage of the technology. This is where we see the greatest discrepancy in the education systems within the United States. The access to rich learning experiences, quality curriculum, and powerful mentors is what is creating the greater divide.

At the same time, access to many of these things is available online in growing measure. A motivated and self-directed young person with a computer and Internet access has what she needs to learn a dozen programming languages, learn about robotics, to connect with people around the world on most any topic of interest, and to leverage a global network of people and resources for personal growth and interest.

The critical issue has to do with how we reimagine education in view of such facts. What does school look like in such a world? How do we create a learning ecosystem that helps more students discover this powerful reality and take advantage of it?

The Good News

With these questions in mind, I will conclude this chapter with one example of an initiative that is tapping into these questions and new realities. In 2014, in partnership with the Mozilla Foundation and a network of entities throughout the city of Chicago, they launched what became the City of Learning.[4] Imagine drawing together all of the different providers of educational experiences across a city: museums, libraries, summer camps and programs, youth agencies, and much more. Now imagine having them connect and collaborate, finding a way to recognize the learning of young people across these organizations with digital badges, potentially even connecting back to the formal curriculum in the public school system. Finally, consider presenting this as a loosely but significantly unified opportunity for learning. They essentially turned the entire city into every young person's classroom. The initiative was so well received that it has now expanded to other cities under the name of the Cities of Learning Connected

4. Chicago Mayor's Press Office, "Mayor Emmanuel Announces."

Learning Alliance.[5] Such an effort points to the emerging possibilities for reimagining education in an increasingly connected world. The time is ripe for hundreds of other such initiatives to surface, allowing us to imagine education in the twenty-first and twenty-second centuries as far from the independent and siloed learning institutions of the past to a massive and global network that leverages partnerships and shared resources to open education in ways rarely imagined in the past.

5. For more information, see http://clalliance.org/cities-of-learning/.

8

Edu-Technopoly

AT A 2006 EDUCAUSE EVENT, Georgia Nugent, then president of Kenyon College, gave a talk entitled "The Tower of Google." It was a thought-provoking presentation, and one of her self-made buzzwords stuck with me. She described her background as a classicist, but also explained her hope for the potential of technology in higher education. She called herself a Luddvocate. This is a word that she uses to describe herself as one who has both concern (the Luddite) and hopes (the advocate) for technology in contemporary society, more specifically education.[1]

I still find that the most intriguing books about technology were written by some of the older self-proclaimed or often labeled Neo-Luddites (people like Lewis Mumford, Marshall McLuhan, Jacques Ellul, Neil Postman, Kirkpatrick Sale, Larry Cuban, and Sven Birkerts). These Neo-Luddites craft messages of caution. They plea for counting the cost of our technological escapades. They challenge the notion that technology is the savior from our greatest social and human needs, and they highlight the adverse impact of technology in society. I read these texts and find myself shouting more than a few inner cheers. These thoughtful texts give a perspective that I believe is valuable and needed in the modern world, especially education. Of course, there are some who, like the original Luddites, turn to violence and destruction

---

1. Nugent, "Tower of Google."

(e.g., Theodore Kaczynski), and I'm quick and clear about rejecting those methods of dissent.

Luddism is not about being anti-technology, in the same way that the Amish are not anti-technology. As I understand them, the Amish are not anti-technology as much as they are pro-community. Similarly, Luddism is about counting the cost of technological progress, not assuming that new technology is always a universal gain for humanity. It is recognizing the values-laden and intrinsically political nature of each technology. New technologies lead to new winners and losers. Luddism champions and gives voice to the losers in the race for technological progress. The original Luddites were moved to action by new machines displacing workers in the textile industry. For the sake of increased productivity, machines replaced people, and that affected their ability to feed their families. Luddism is about challenging us to be users of technologies instead of passively allowing ourselves to be used by them.

Then there is the advocate. While I'm not sure how Nugent might further extrapolate on what it means to be an advocate, I confess that I originally became one because I didn't think I had much of a choice. Just like the original Luddites lost their fight against the vision of progress brought about by the Industrial Revolution, I suspect that many Neo-Luddites will experience the same. What is a person to do? I distinctly remember struggling with this question throughout the middle of the 1990s, with my first regional presentation being about the negative impact of technology in education at an educational technology conference in Chicago. I still remember the line of software vendors glaring at me with their arms crossed along the back of the surprisingly standing-room-only session. I quoted Neil Postman freely as I warned about the "Faustian bargain" of new technologies. Postman explained it in *The End of Education* this way:

> All technological change is a Faustian bargain. For every advantage a new technology offers, there is always a corresponding disadvantage.[2]

---

2. Postman, *End of Education*, 192.

The title of this chapter is a play on the title of Neil Postman's book *Technopoly*, where he uses the term to describe instances where a "culture seeks its authorization in technology, finds its satisfactions in technology, and takes its orders from technology."[3] I simply use "edu-technopoly" to refer to instances where this same thing happens within school cultures and contexts—instances where technology drives the decisions instead of serving as a diverse collection of tools to help achieve the goals of the school, purse the mission, and live out the values of the organization. An edu-technopoly is at work when the technology itself is intentionally or unknowing put in a place of authority above mission, vision, values, and goals.

It is unrealistic and ultimately unhelpful, however, to simply reject technological developments in education. We have a much better chance if we simply strive to influence which technologies to amplify and which to muffle. I called it values-driven decision making. Identify your core values and convictions and let them drive your decisions about technology. Once you have clarity about those core convictions, you will be able to decide where, how, when, and about what to advocate. I felt good about my talk, hoping that it resonated with the attendees, until the first question during the question-and-answer period. It was a principal wanting a list of the best software to use in his kindergarten classes. So much for values driving the decisions. I learned early on that technology in education had become a value of its own.

I found that many of my concerns about technology were connected to what I considered to be dehumanizing effects of the Industrial Revolution. Don't get me wrong. I like many of the benefits of the Industrial Revolution. It is just that I had and have hope that emerging democratizing technology might assist us in mitigating against some of the negative aspects of that era.

I had visions of *Brave New World*, *1984*, *The Giver*, and dozens of other dystopian stories of our future. So I chose to advocate for technology that seems to amplify values of democracy, access, and opportunity. It is what inspires me about the possibilities of

3. Postman, *Technopoly*, 71.

everything from blended learning to online learning, alternative education to self-directed learning, open education to open badges and micro-credentials, personalized learning to adaptive learning software, project-based learning to social media, personal learning networks to communities of practice. It is why I can geek out about designing high-impact online learning communities while being a passionate supporter of existing and emerging physical third spaces (thank you Ray Oldenburg[4]) that conjure a spirit of community. It is why I lobby for choice and variety in options for formal education. It is why I have degrees in both the humanities and instructional technology. It is why I am a champion for formal higher education while calling for those same institutions to resist the temptation to claim a monopoly on learning and knowledge, as if either were a commodity to be bought and sold.

Each of these represent deep-seated personal values and convictions about truth, beauty, goodness, purpose, and what it means to be human. It shapes how I write and speak about the future, both forecasting and striving to create or influence possible futures. Ironically, it is the Luddite in me that drives me to be such an advocate for life and learning in the digital world. The Luddite is the one who cries out that our ideas have consequences, our convictions matter, human access and opportunity are noble causes, and that all three should inform the futures that we help create.

Why This Is a Critical Issue

Is technology a neutral tool or does it have implications for fundamental questions about curriculum studies and the mission, vision, values, and goals of contemporary educational institutions? How does technology shape our schools, curricula, teachers, students, and leaders? With the growth of technology integration, blended learning, online learning, and a myriad of applications of technology in education, this chapter provides a set of definitions

4. See Oldenburg, *Great Good Place*.

and three starting points for deeper reflection about such questions, considering the affordances and limitations of technology in modern education, challenging scholars and practitioners to consider the values amplified and minimized by various technological decisions.

Technology Is Values Laden[5]

If you ever attended a presentation on educational technology, there is a good chance that you heard the presenter make the comment, "It is not about the technology." Such presenters usually continue by claiming that "technology is just a neutral tool." This neutral-tool approach to describing technology makes intuitive sense, but it also risks missing several important facts about the role of technology in life and learning. As a result, following is a definition of technology that has promise to serve us in thinking more deeply about the nature and role of technology in education, as well as give us an important clarification about a philosophy of educational technology.

If technology is just a tool, what is a tool? Here is one common definition: "a device or implement, especially one held in the hand, used to carry out a particular function: 'gardening tools.'"[6] In other words, specific tools are created for specific uses and not other ones; they have biases toward some applications and away from others. What would it mean for us to claim that a hammer is just a tool, and that it all depends upon how we use it? By this, we might mean that it is not the fault of the hammer if someone happens to use it to hit another person on the head. However, most hammers are created to hit things. In fact, different hammers are created to hit different things. While it is not the intent of a hammer to hit a person on the head, one is more likely to do that with

5. A large portion of this section is revised and used with permission from a monograph that I published in 2016, entitled "Teaching the Faith, Technology, and Education."

6. Oxford Dictionaries, "Tool." http://www.oxforddictionaries.com/us/definition/american_english/tool.

unpleasant results than if the same person were holding a pillow. This is why we are more comfortable letting small children play with pillows than we are with hammers.

This example has other important elements. Some hammers have intended uses beyond hitting things as well. A ball-peen hammer, for example, was not created for the same purpose as a carpenter's hammer. Or consider the fact that a gavel, a judge's hammer, is mostly a communication tool. Imagine using a gavel to help build a birdhouse, or a judge opting to use a sledgehammer instead of a gavel. While it might reinforce the judge's authority, it might also put a hole in the desk.

Is technology neutral? Is it just about how a person uses the technology? Or does the design of the technology itself impact how one uses it? The hammer illustrations seem to reveal that technologies have affordances (benefits) and limitations, a concept articulated more fully in several of Neil Postman's texts. Technology makes certain things possible and more likely. As a result, when something is more possible, we tend to think about that possibility. Sitting in front of a block of concrete that needs removal with a ball-peen hammer in one's hand will not lead most of us to start chipping the pavement. Sitting in the same place with a sledgehammer is far more likely to lead and inspire one to think about taking a swing. The affordances of a technology lead us to consider possibilities that were otherwise hidden. Similarly, technologies have limitations. The limitations of a ball-peen hammer includes the fact that it is not an especially useful tool for a person needing to break up a concrete block.

Perhaps a different definition will help us think more broadly about technology in life and learning. Technology can be understood as applied systematic knowledge. We discover something, learn about how it works or functions, and then use that knowledge to design a tool or collection of tools to help solve one or more real-world problems. That design is a technology, knowledge applied to meet a need in the world. A carpenter needs to find a way to attach different types of wood. As human knowledge progressed, people invented nails and hammers as technologies to help accomplish such tasks. To say that hammers and nails are just neutral tools would not make sense in this context. The tool was created to solve a specific problem. Hammers like nails more than screws. It is not just about how the wielder of the hammer desires to use it. Regardless of the user's skill or intent, hammering screws will produce unhelpful results. If an uninformed aspiring carpenter sought to ignore such facts, the results of trying to drive a screw into two pieces of wood would have an evident and qualitatively different end.

With this said, it is possible to "hack" a problem with a hammer—a term with new connotations in some aspects of popular culture.[7] A hacker can be seen as a person who uses technologies and resources in unexpected and often creative ways, using a tool to solve a problem for which it was not intended. One might, for example, use three hammers to entertain someone by showing how a skilled person can juggle them. One might be locked in a room and use an available hammer to break out of the room.

While it is possible to ignore the intended purpose of a given technology, things do not always work out. We might fail in these efforts, or we might succeed only to find one or more unintended consequences. One can use a sledgehammer to solve a finish carpentry problem, but it might leave a few more dents and scratches than if one used the tool designed for the job.

Implications for Education

What does this extended example have to do with education and schooling in a technological age? Following are three potential applications. First, our definition of technology is too narrow, not leading us to consider the full impact of our technological decisions in schools. Second, if technologies have intended uses, we are wise to get informed about those uses, learning about the affordances and limitations of the technologies in our schools and lives. Third, current educational technologies are not as simple as

7. Urban Dictionary, "Hack." http://www.urbandictionary.com/define.php?term=hack.

the hammer example. Their intended uses are not as transparent. However, thoughtful reflection can help us to make wise decisions.

Broadening Our Definition

If we accepted the proposal of a broader definition for technology, that it is applied systematic knowledge, we soon discover ourselves surrounded by technologies, even in what we otherwise thought as the most low-tech school or classroom. While many think of technology in terms of computers, this broader definition invites us to think about thousands of educational technologies in our schools: bell schedules, pens, school desks, the configuration of classrooms, school architecture, grading systems, lesson plan templates, textbooks, curricula, even school policies and classroom management models. Inventors of such things gathered existing knowledge on the subject, organized it, and designed something to address a specific problem. Of course, technology also includes things like the Internet and the devices we use to connect to it, interactive whiteboards, cell phones, and Web-based software and tools.

This broader definition of technology shows that educational technology and schools are inseparable. There are few examples of schools today that do not make heavy use of educational technology. Even the way that we separate subjects is a technology. Consider the fact that many study social studies as a distinct subject from science, math separate from language arts, and art separate from physical education. These are inventions and conventions, not discoveries. They are taxonomies and organizational systems to help us categorize knowledge. This leaves us with a significant challenge and opportunity to better understand how all these technologies influence the mission, vision, values, and goals of a given learning community.

Exploring Intended Uses, Affordances and Limitations[8]

With this broad definition of educational technology, we have the challenge and opportunity for reflection and study about the intended uses, affordances, and limitations of them. Interestingly, there are no books (books, by the way, are an educational technology) that address the broad spectrum of school technologies in this way. We are often left to do our own homework (homework is also an educational technology). Such an exercise is not something that is easily addressed by reading a quick resource on the subject. Instead, we find ourselves needing to research, to find lesser known and referenced resources. Consider, for example, the fact that the contemporary letter grade system is, in the big picture, a young technology. Scan resources on the history of letter grades, and we find claims that they were first used in the United States in the early to middle nineteenth century.[9] Prior to that, much American education did not use the letter grade system. Taking the example of the educational technology known as the letter grade system, we then have the challenge of figuring out the intended use of the letter grade system, reflecting on the affordances of such a system, as well as the limitations of it. Only when we engage in such work do we begin to discover how this technology helps and hinders our deepest beliefs and values associated with schools in a specific time and location.

Neil Postman suggested that we ask the question, "What is the problem to which this technology is the solution"?[10] Consider that question with the grading system. What problem was the grading system created to solve? Does that problem still exist today? Is it the best solution available to us? Are there potentially alternative

8. As with the last section, a large portion of this section is revised and used with permission from a monograph that I published in 2015 entitled "Teaching the Faith, Technology, and Education."

9. Cureton, "History of Grading Practices," 1–8.

10. Postman, "Technology and Society," at 2:00 in part 2 of the YouTube posting.

solutions that better align with our distinct mission, vision, values, and goals in education?

Complexity with Technology and Education[11]

This concept of affordances and limitations is distinct from asking about what is good or bad. This study of the affordances and limitations recognizes that there are always benefits and limits to any technology. No single technology is free from downsides. As such, it becomes important to spend time in reflection, study, and collaboration with colleagues that help us become more informed about these matters. For example, using devices connected to the Internet as part of formal schooling can be justified in many ways. We return to Neil Postman's question, "What is the problem to which this technology is the solution?" I will add a second question to that: "What are the possibilities made available by this technology?" Asking these and similar questions to educators, learners, and other stakeholders is likely to produce different answers. We might hear responses like:

- Using such tools and technology is an important public relations and marketing strategy, so that people see us as providing a comparable education to the public schools.

- It gives us access to an unprecedented amount of free resources.

- It helps us equip students for the nature of life in a connected world.

- It allows us to create more customized and personalized learning experiences for students, which further helps us embrace our call to meet the unique needs of each learner and not teach all learners as if they were the same.

- It engages students who grew up in the digital world.

11. As with the last two sections, a large portion of this section is revised and used with permission from a monograph that I published in 2015 entitled "Teaching the Faith, Technology, and Education."

- It allows us to connect with people and resources around the world, discovering more diverse perspectives and ideas in the world.

One need not agree with each of these reasons, but these are the types of affordances that people might point to when thinking about the adoption of a given technology or set of educational technologies. Getting informed about such affordances allows for more thoughtful decisions.

Similarly, it is beneficial to recognize the limitations and the biases associated with them. Sticking with the example of devices connected to the Internet, people might share one or more of the following limitations:

- It is expensive and takes away from investments in other aspects of education.

- It exposes young people to inappropriate content and resources.

- It can turn the classroom into something that focuses on "bells and whistles" and less on the important skills and content.

- It leads to classroom management problems.

- It contributes to young people who are more connected to devices than they are to people in front of them.

- It promotes a digital divide between students with rich technology resources at home and those who do not have Internet access in their homes.

Again, the items in these incomplete lists are debatable. Nonetheless, they help us become more informed and intentional about our choices. They guide us through thinking about the ways in which we use and apply technology to pursue our mission, vision, values, and goals in a specific learning organization as well as the broader field of education.

It is less advisable to rush ahead with educational technologies, while labeling those with questions and concerns as Luddites or self-serving. Read about the history of writing, and we find grave concerns from people like Socrates, who believed that writing would dull the memory. Of course, it was writing that allows us to even know that Socrates supposedly made such a claim. Yet, Socrates was correct. The art of memory is less prevalent and emphasized by people today.[12] That is an accurate limitation of embracing such a technology. Nonetheless, most Americans are likely to find that the affordances of writing as a technology outweigh the limitations. In other words, we move forward in the reflective and thoughtful use of technologies, but do not move forward blindly or uninformed. We listen and learn from different perspectives, carefully considering affordances and limitations.

Even with such careful study, there can be unexpected consequences to educational technology decisions. As noted before, there are always benefits and limitations. Over time these unexpected consequences become apparent to us. Consider the massive media about the failed 2013 iPad initiative in the Los Angeles public schools. This is a well-resourced team of decision-makers, and yet several challenges emerged that led them to cancel the program and collect all of the iPads they had recently distributed to each student.[13]

Given the inevitability of unexpected consequences, how do we prepare for this? This brings us back to the mission, vision, values, and goals of the school. With any new innovation or educational technology adoption, it becomes important to start with a plan to collect data about how things are going, what is working well, and what is not working well. In other words, the challenge of examining the affordances and limitations is not simply something that we do in advance of adopting a new technology. It is important to continue to explore this, even as we adopt and use a given technology. Consider the following questions and how a school or teacher might go about collecting data on these questions in an ongoing way.

12. Foer, *Moonwalking with Einstein*, 139–40.
13. Gilbertson, "Few LA Students Using Pearson's iPad Software."

- What is working and what is not?

- If there are problems, it is inherent to the technology or is to more related to how we are using it?

- Are we noticing any unexpected consequences?

- How is this helping to increase student learning?

- What inequities are minimized or amplified?

- How is it helping us to pursue our mission, vision, values, and goals?

- How is this technology changing the way that teachers teach and students learn?

- What are the benefits and drawbacks to these changes?

- What is this technology amplifying and what it is minimizing?

- Are the benefits worth the cost of this investment?

- What adjustments could be made to make this work better?

- Are there any students who are not benefitting or are being harmed from this new technology adoption?

Learning from Neil Postman

While I never met him face to face, Neil Postman (in the form of his writings) was my tutor when it came to thinking about media and culture. I'm the first to admit that Postman would have likely disapproved of much that occupies my thought, work, and time today. I am, in many ways, a contributor to what he described as a *Technopoly*. Nonetheless, Postman left a mark on me when it comes to considering the importance of media literacy, exploring how technology "uses us," and in the call to equip youth with the ability to ask and find answers to the difficult and often unasked questions about the Faustian bargains present with each new technology. His framework for critiquing technology in society and education more specifically remains a light to guide us through the present of future of learning in a digital and connected world.

As we learned about the ever-increasing amount of information that is available to the typical person over the past decade, Postman was quick to point out that more information is hardly ever the answer to problems in the modern world. We have plenty of information, he would explain—more than one individual could possibly use. For that reason, Postman distinguished between information, knowledge, and wisdom. Knowledge is the logical organization of information; it is making sense and meaning out of the individual bits of information. And wisdom is capacity to use the knowledge in order to make the best decisions, to choose one path over another.[14]

I often wonder what Postman would have to say about some of the technologies emerging in the last few years as well as some of the efforts to help make sense of, organize, and visually represent what was previously just an earth-sized ball of knotted strings of information. Perhaps he would point out that these are rarely true moves toward knowledge or wisdom, but just information about information—lots of form with minimal substance. Or, it may be that he would accept that these are moves toward knowledge, but he might just return to some of his famous questions. What problem is this information technology solving? Who are the winners and losers when this technology is used? What are the unexpected consequences of these technologies?[15]

For me, these questions are not a call to cease innovation (as if anyone other than a few friends with a horse a buggy would listen), but rather a challenge for us to bridge the gap between our technological advancements and our humanity, a call to remember that ideas have consequences, that ethics are important, and that humanity has a responsibility to pursue that which is good, pure, noble, true, and right—especially when we are talking about a subject as important as education.

14. Postman, "Infoming Ourselves to Death," para. 10.
15. See Postman, "Technology and Society."

9

Vocation and Good Work

THERE IS SO MUCH we can learn from young people. It is why I appreciate Howard Rheinhold's approach when he refers to his students as colearners. I was reminded of what we can learn from young people as I read an article by Velammal Vidhyashram, an eight-grader who lives in Chennai, the capitol city of Tamil Nadu, in southern India.[1] Velemmal is a motivated and accomplished young man, already running his own business. However, what impressed me about the article was his perspective on life and his advice to other young people. He finished the article by writing:

> My message to other young people is this: "Look for problems around you, and get inspired from them. You'll see a lot of opportunities to use your [own] skills to make this world a better place to live!"[2]

I'm intrigued by this simple approach to loving his fellow neighbors in our global neighborhood. I'm also intrigued by how the three parts of his advice set the foundation for a wonderfully rich approach to education.

---

1. Vidhyashram, "No Kidding."
2. Ibid.

1) "Look for Problems"[3]

What are the needs in the world? What about your local world? What are the problems that impact the people in your family, community, state, country, and world? Start by learning about the needs that exist. While many state these as problems, I also like to think of it as exploring both the problems and the possibilities in the world.

2) "Get Inspired from Them"[4]

As you consider these problems, which ones inspire you? Which ones capture your interest and compel you to do something about them? I like a term shared by Bill Hybels; he calls it *Holy Discontent*.[5] This need not be some great awakening or a "road to Damascus" experience. It might just be a real need in the world that you care about, something that inspires you to act.

3) "Use Your Skills to Improve the World"[6]

Now that you've identified a problem, do something about it. If you already have knowledge and skills that can be used to help address the problem, by all means, use them. Or, perhaps you find that you need to gain more knowledge, develop new skills, or build up existing ones. Go for it. This is a wonderful motivation for learning.

Some approach a phrase like "improve the world" with skepticism. The world is a big place and there is so much wrong with it. The danger is to become immersed in such a mindset set so much that it overwhelms and leads us toward inaction. You don't have to save the world. Just think of specific people who have the need that you identified, and learn to help them. As one very wise person said, "Love your neighbor as yourself" (Mark 12:31).

3. Ibid.
4. Ibid.
5. See Hybels, *Holy Discontent*.
6. Vidhyashram, "No Kidding."

Which Neighbors in This World Need Your Help?

While this is a rich perspective on life, it is also a compelling vision for schooling. What if learners were invited to spend part of their time in school working through these three steps? 1) Identify a problem. 2) Grow in your passion for and interest in that problem. 3) Use or gain the knowledge and skills needed to do something about it, then do it. This could be a beautifully simple but profound way for young people to spend part of their school day. I'm not talking about a teacher playing a video about starving children and then having the kids put together care packages. While that may be admirable, I'm referring to an invitation for each student to identity a problem or need, and work toward addressing it. Along the way, students will likely need to gain new knowledge and skill, and this becomes a generative curriculum.

This is not to suggest that all schools should become full self-directed learning centers. I'm simply arguing for setting aside part of the school day for this type of experience. What do you think? Is there room in our packed school days and curricula for students to invest a little time in addressing the needs of the world?

This points us to the critical issue of this chapter: the idea of vocation and good work. As with the chapter on purpose and meaning, it is too easy for us to focus on the individual elements of education—the rules and regulations, requirements for external compliance, earning a certain grade, or any number of other factors. Yet, none of these add rich purpose or meaning to the education enterprise. On the other hand, a concept like calling offers something more compelling upon which to build an engaging education enterprise.

Lessons from Mr. Rogers

Several years ago, inspired by a blog post from Chris Brogan, I decided to abandon my standard New Year's resolution, instead opting to select three words to direct my work and thought.[7] In

7. Brogan, "My Three Words for 2013."

2014, two of my words were Frost was Rogers. I chose to spend the year learning more about two people, Robert Frost and Fred (Mr.) Rogers. Why Mr. Rogers? Yes, I watched his show as a child, and I have fond memories of it. However, it is also because of the philosophy of life that he embraced and the way he determined how to invest his time and energy. Consider the following diagram that is based upon what Joanne Rogers (his wife) described in the foreword to *Life's Journeys According to Mr. Rogers*. She noted that ". . . he knew in his heart that there could be a connection between television, the real needs of human beings (particularly children), and spirituality."[8] These three items combined to become what we now remember as *Mister Rogers' Neighborhood*.

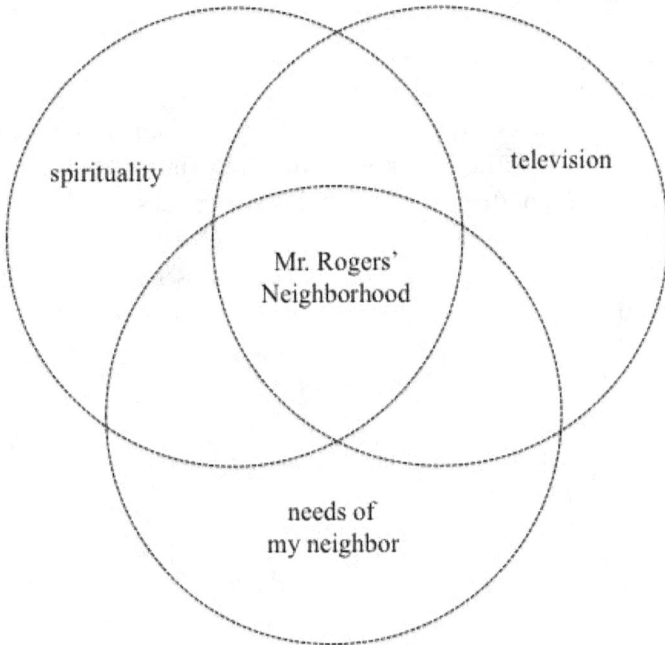

spirituality

television

Mr. Rogers' Neighborhood

needs of my neighbor

8. Rogers, *Life's Journeys According to Mr. Rogers*, iii.

Television (The Dominant Technology of His Day)

According to Joanne, already in college Fred had a fascination with the technology of television. He was troubled by some of the uses of this media, but also believed it had great promise for good, granted that one designed something properly. He invested years of his life into studying and developing the skills necessary to flourish in the television industry. This included entry jobs over the years that eventually led to doing puppetry, running a lesser-known show on a Canadian TV station, and finally becoming known as the face and mind behind *Mister Rogers' Neighborhood*.

The Real Needs of Human Beings

The second core conviction was a desire to do good. In an interview, Fred described how his mother dealt with seeing tragedies and unpleasant events in the world. She said to him, "Always look for the helpers."[9] This means not getting drawn into the depression and darkness of the bad events, but devoting one's energy to the needs of people in those events, and the people who are getting involved and striving to meet those needs. In essence, it is a worldview that looks for the people who are striving to be a neighbor to those in need, to find real needs of people and then to meet them using your distinct gifts and abilities.

Spirituality

It is well known that Fred Rogers was a man of faith and had a seminary degree. While he was not explicit about the source of his beliefs and values in his show, they informed the words that he used, the way he treated people, and the type of show he hosted. While I have no direct evidence, it would not be a stretch to suggesting that the idea of *Mister Rogers' Neighborhood* was not just about a traditional concept of being in a neighborhood, but was

9. Rogers, interview.

drawing upon the foundational Christian teaching, "Love your neighbor as yourself" (Mark 12:31). For some Christians, this is a source text for a large idea that we sometimes refer to as vocation or calling: using one's unique combination of gifts, talents, abilities, and context to show love for one's many neighbors in the world.

These three values of Fred Rogers intersected to shape his life's work, *Mister Rogers' Neighborhood*. They help us understand the why behind the work of Mr. Rogers. They also give us a guide and potential template for thinking about our own life's work.

Interestingly, this is part of why I elected to spend more time learning about Fred Rogers. Soon after college, I too became intrigued by the increasingly dominant technology of my age, the Internet. I also shared a common core of Christian spirituality, and part of my tradition holds love for neighbor in high regard, as a foundational teaching in discovering one's callings in life. As a result, I thought that I could learn from a person who is highly regarded and unquestioningly impactful in his work.

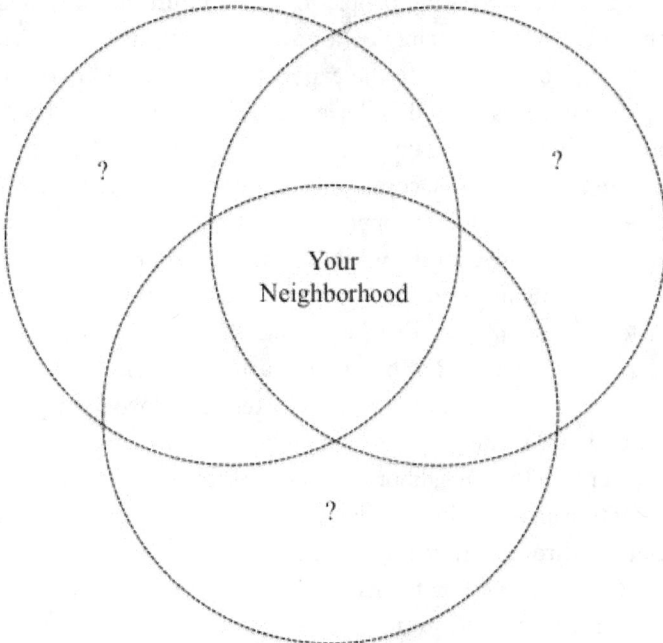

Learning organizations can use this simple guide to help students clarify, discover, or explore their own callings in life. As we explored in an earlier chapter, this gives even greater significance to a question like, "What gifts, talents, interests, and abilities do I have that might benefit the needs of people in the world?" By identifying something for the two or three circles in the Venn diagram, perhaps it will help us to discover our neighborhood(s), that place(s) where our gifts, passions, and interests intersect with the needs of people in the world.

Consider how this framework might serve as a guide for learning organizations. What if the fundamental purpose of a learning organization were to help people refine their neighborhood, and then to develop the knowledge and skills necessary to thrive in meeting the needs of people in that neighborhood? That makes for a compelling why to drive the experiments and innovations of learning organizations in the twenty-first century.

While this is a powerful way for thinking about future callings, it also works for the present. School doesn't need to be exclusively about preparing people for some future set of callings, although that can certainly be a powerful motivator and means of adding rich meaning to the experience. We can think of calling in many ways. We might have callings to certain career paths and jobs, but also to many roles in life, like mother, father, son, daughter, brother, sister, community member, and even the role of student. Each of these are opportunities to leverage our time and talents to show love for the neighbors in those contexts.

With this in mind, a fundamental calling that we too often fail to address in school is the calling of student. What does it mean to be a student? What is the purpose of being a student? Or, from the notion that calling is interested in love of neighbor, how to do we invite students to grapple with questions about how they can love their neighbor through their calling as student, not to mention an even more fundamental question. If I am to love my neighbor through my calling as a student, who is my neighbor?

Certainly one way to answer this question is to focus on the future. I devote myself to my studies so that I am better prepared to love the neighbors in my future callings in life. Wouldn't the world be better off if future doctors devoted themselves to personal growth and development in school, with the idea that their studies and preparation could leave them either prepared or ill-prepared for life-and-death moments of their future patients? In other words, my neighbors in my calling as a student are all whom I might serve and support with the knowledge and abilities that I develop.

This applies for the one who has a clear vision for a future profession, but also the people who has no idea what they might do in the future. If we don't know what the future holds, how much more important is it for us to embrace all of our studies, as we do not yet know what we will need. There is a sense of responsibility that comes with a student's studies because, while she might pursue her personal interests in the present, if she is willing to accept that her life exists not only for her benefit but for the benefit of others, then she understands that her present efforts impact her future accomplishments.

This is, of course, not an easy concept for the youngest of people to grasp. I don't expect every fifth-grader to avoid procrastinating on a homework assignment because she has a vivid picture of the people she will serve with her knowledge in two decades. Despite that reality, this is indeed a valuable perspective for us to introduce and reinforce throughout education. A sense of calling nurtures a sense of meaning and purpose. It adds weight to the why of education.

At the same time, the vocation of student can draw students to be more invested their present. This might seem strange because it is such an unfamiliar line of thinking in much of modern education, but I invite the reader to bracket judgments for just a moment and consider the possibilities. Who are the other neighbors in a learning context as one lives out the calling of student? Consider that classmates, teachers, community members, and even the authors of texts are neighbors to be loved through the calling of student.

If I see my classmates as neighbors to love, how will that impact my approach to and perspective on education? Considering these classmates as neighbors, and one's calling to them makes education a true community effort. It means that it is not just about students learning for their own good, but for them to invest in helping others learn and find joy in their learning.

There are neighbors in the world and in the community who can benefit even in the present tense through students efforts as well. This is where a concept like service learning has great potential. With service learning, one integrates a substantive act of service in the community with the formal curriculum. It isn't just volunteering at a soup kitchen, but it is using content area knowledge and learning in a way that serves people in the community. It adds a compelling sense of relevance to what one is studying and casts a vision for how the content can be used for good in the world.

Then there are the neighbors who are teachers. Consider a school context where teachers see students as neighbors to be loved and served, and the students see teachers as neighbors to love as well. This sets the stage for a powerful mentoring and coaching relationship that can be mutually beneficial. There is this mutual commitment to listening to and learning from one another. There is a shared commitment to exploring a topic of interest and using it for good. It shifts away from a power differential and toward a true learning community, where everyone sees their role and responsibility to the others in the community. Having visited many learning organizations around the world, it takes very little time to recognize this sort of a culture when you step into such a learning organization. A group of people who are invested in their community and callings make for an incredibly positive learning environment.

Even the books that we read and resources that we use have neighbors to love. When I read a book, I recognize that it was written by people who were living out one of their callings as a writer, author, or teacher. I honor them by sacrificing precious time in my life to read and reflect on what they write. I "listen" carefully to what they say. I take what is useful and good. I respectfully leave behind what might be less useful. Nonetheless, this sort of humanizing approach to using books and educational resources adds even more meaning to the experience. It adds honor to the exchange and can cultivate a sense of wonder and gratitude in even the simplest of learning experiences, like curling up on a couch and reading a book.

I am convinced that the concept of calling is a powerful lever for infusing meaning and purpose into our learning organizations, as I referenced in a previous chapter. It gives people a sense of direction. It nurtures hope. It taps into something that is wonderfully human, intellectually stimulating, and it inspires people toward action and progress.

10

Truth, Beauty, Goodness

FACULTY ARE NERVOUS, AT LEAST SOME of them. The higher education headlines highlight questions about online learning, the affordability of higher education, open learning, high school/college dual-credit programs, competency-based education, alternate credentials, and a growing focus on workforce development and professional programs. Amid such changes, I see a growing number of faulty, especially those in the humanities and liberal arts, speaking up about what is lost with each of these areas, even while others in the liberal arts are among some of the greatest champions for one or more of these developments. I read heartfelt as well as carefully thought-out responses to these movements, and there is much to learn from such texts.

The case for the liberal arts has not changed significantly over the years. The liberal arts prepare literate and thinking people. They seek to cultivate good citizens who will promote and uphold the principles of a democracy. They equip one to fully embrace the life of a free person. They help one explore the life of truth, beauty, and goodness. It is not difficult to agree with such outcomes. However, are we talking about the liberal arts or a formal liberal arts curriculum? Are they the same? Were they the same for people in the past?

Consider some of the texts that will be read in many formal liberal arts curricula. They are texts from antiquity, and often more recent literary works. Among many others, one is likely to read Whitman, Hemingway, Shaw, Salinger, Sandberg, Tolstoy, Faulkner, Frost, Twain, Blake, and Austin. Interestingly, what these authors share in common is no formal college liberal arts education. The student of history and government will study US presidents like Washington, Van Buren, Lincoln, Taylor, Cleveland, and Truman as well. None of these people had a formal college education either, with Washington, Lincoln, and Johnson having only one year of any formal education between the three of them. Yet many of these people had liberal arts influences. Many read widely and nurtured disciplined habits of the mind that we might associate with a liberally educated person. They were self-directed and lifelong learners who read, wrote, spoke, and lived the principles often identified with a liberal arts education. Is this what we really want—not just people with liberal arts credentials, but people who live with a liberal arts worldview?

The liberal arts are about more than courses, credits, degrees, and programs. As such, perhaps the debate for a formal liberal arts education is not as critical as one about the importance of the liberal arts in an individual's life and community. In other words, if one truly wants to defend the value of the liberal arts, then perhaps there is need to think more broadly than formal schooling, instead looking at ways to encourage and nurture a value for the liberal arts in the world beyond school. It is one thing to read Chaucer to pass the quiz, test, or class; it is another to read such a book in the evening after a long day of work.

Neither K–12 schools nor the universities own the liberal arts, nor does any particular school or department of a university, for example. By narrowing the debate about the liberal arts to the method of learning, or to formal programming, we may risk losing the spirit of the liberal arts. The liberal arts are about knowledge, skill, and disposition. The *how* is not as central. It might be for some proponents of formal classical education, but not as much for the broader community of liberal arts advocates.

If the debate is really an economic one, with employees of liberal arts programs fighting for the viability of their jobs and programs, that is one thing. Yet, it is a qualitatively different thing to discuss the value of a liberally educated person, one who has thought deeply about matters of truth, beauty, and goodness. One can shared that value without necessarily advocating that more people should study at liberal arts colleges or pursue liberal arts degrees, or that a formal liberal arts education is worth the cost. In other words, for the sake of the liberal arts in contemporary society, I suggest that it is time to carefully separate the two. Both are worthwhile discussions, but the program is not the only possible route to promoting the liberal arts. In fact, I suspect that investing more time, energy, and resources into the promotion of the liberal arts in society may well benefit the programs. Just look at what CSI did to criminal justice and forensics programs, or what Indiana Jones did for archeology programs in the past. After all, I'm pretty sure that Shakespeare didn't get his start in the lecture halls, but rather in the public square (or rather the theater).

Truth, beauty, and goodness are all around us. They are not limited to formal study in the lecture halls. What is true? What is beautiful? What is good? These are not questions that we want to lock away in formal schooling, but questions that we are wise to discuss throughout society. When there is a political campaign, this is a prime time to be relentless in our pursuit of and commitment to conversations about truth and goodness. When we discuss film and literature, these three questions are present as well. As we work through difficulties and challenging decisions in our lives, don't these questions come to us again?

Truth, beauty, and goodness are too important to be limited to formal schooling. They are foundations to our well-being in our individual lives, our families, our communities, our nation, and our world. They help us discover many of the other matters explored in this book, topics like calling, purpose, mission, agency, humanity, even what it means to be educated.

At the same time, these are certainly ideas that have incredible power and promise in shaping our vision for formal education. Truth, beauty, and goodness; along with other ideas like justice and equality, these are ideas that have the depth to inspire a great education, granted that we do not dissect them or constrict them by some of the unnecessary restraints already mentioned in this book. These are ideas that have near limitless depth for the deepest of thinkers but simultaneously offer more shallow waters for the newcomer. They are pools from which we can return countless times, never finding the pail empty.

Of course, not everyone is tolerant of such grand ideas. Our contemporary conversations about education are often more grounded in debates about what some consider more practical or pressing matters. These are matters like workforce development, the cost of higher education, holding teachers and institutions accountable, keeping the budget in check, comparing students around the world on some common numeric scale, or winning some supposed global competition.

Indeed, these are all real issues that warrant serious debate and decisions. Yet, how much richer would these conversations be if we invested ourselves in inviting true and open study and conversation of these more foundational principles like truth, beauty, goodness, justice, and others? Instead, we too often skip them, opting to spend almost all of our time defending our group or agenda, positioning ourselves for victory in the debate, fighting in the battle for resources or power, lobbying for our causes.

While formal educational institutions are not adequate for these conversations, nor should they claim a corner on the market for them, they nonetheless play an important role in society. Even amid the many trends and contemporary issues that I have addressed in this text, I contend that these more classical ideals for education continue to have value. Formal schools can be places where these ideas are taken seriously, where teachers and students struggle with them, where civil discourse is modeled and nurtured, and where ideas that have grand implications are studied, celebrated, and spread. Any book about critical issues in education is lacking if it does not return to these foundations.

If formal education ceases to be about truth, beauty, and goodness, it will soon lose its relevance in society. It will wither alongside anything else that fails to drink from the well of such important ideals. In a world of high-stakes testing and credentialism, these ideas can give us balance and perspective. In a world thirst-ing for meaning and purpose, they offer us our fill of both. In a world battling over the value and dignity of individuals and their agency, these ideals give us at least common ground upon which to discuss. In an increasingly connected and digital world, with its associated benefits and limitations, questions about truth, beauty, and goodness draw us back to questions about humanity. In a world where research is directing us back to the fact that char-acter and non-cognitive skills matter; these ideas are central to the conversation. And in a world where people struggles to find their place in the world, their distinct callings, are we not wise to consider what is true, good, and beautiful in our lives and what we do with them? If any of these other issues are critical, then so are truth, beauty, and goodness.

Bibliography

Andrade, Heidi L., and Gregory J. Cizek. *Handbook of Formative Assessment.* New York: Routledge, 2010.

Belfied, Clive, and Peter Crosta. "Predicting Success in College: The Importance of Placement Tests and High School Transcripts." Community College Research Center. February 2012. http://ccrc.tc.columbia.edu/media/k2/attachments/predicting-success-placement-tests-transcripts.pdf.

Bingham, Charles. "Why We Should Shred Our Diplomas." November 24, 2014. https://www.youtube.com/watch?v=MWoLiYQZmZQ.

Bower, Joe, and P. L. Thomas. *De-Testing and De-Grading Schools: Authentic Alternatives to Accountability and Standardization.* New York: Peter Lang, 2013.

Bridgeland, John M., et al. "The Silent Epidemic: Perspectives of High School Dropouts." Civic Enterprises. March 2006. http://www.civicenterprises.net/MediaLibrary/Docs/the_silent_epidemic.pdf.

Brogan, Chris. "My Three Words for 2013." January 2013. http://chrisbrogan.com/my-3-words-for-2013/.

Brown, Sally. "Let's Make It Fair." *Independent,* May 8, 1996. http://www.independent.co.uk/news/education/education-news/lets-make-it-fair-1346381.html

Bull, Bernard. "Credentials, Gatekeepers, & Openness in Education." December 11, 2014. http://etale.org/main/2014/12/11/credentials-gatekeepers-openness-in-education/.

———. "Good Teachers Become Less Important." April 9, 2009. http://etale.org/main/2013/04/09/good-teachers-need-to-become-less-important/.

———. *Missional Moonshots: Insights and Inspiration for Educational Innovation.* Greenwood, WI: Athanathos, 2016.

———. "Teaching the Faith, Technology, and Education." LEA eMonograph. River Forest, IL: Lutheran Education Association, 2016. http://www.lea.org/Portals/10/Monographs/FaithTechnologyTeaching.pdf?ver=2016-02-26-155916-257.

————. "25 Must-Read Books for the Educational Hacktivist or Contrarian." December 9, 2014. http://etale.org/main/2014/12/09/25-must-read-books-for-the-educational-hacktivist-or-contrarian/.

Chicago Mayor's Press Office. "Mayor Emanuel Announces Expanded Citywide Summer of Learning and Earning Initiative with Over 10,000 Additional Learning and Employment Opportunities for Chicago Youth." April 2014. http://www.cityofchicago.org/city/en/depts/mayor/press_room/press_releases/2014/apr/mayor-emanuel-announces-expanded-citywide-summer-of-learning-and.html.

Church, Kathryn. *Forbidden Narratives: Critical Autobiography as Social Science.* Australia: Gordon and Breach, 1995.

Crow, Dan. "Why Every Child Should Learn to Code." *The Guardian*, February 7, 2014. https://www.theguardian.com/technology/2014/feb/07/year-of-code-dan-crow-songkick.

Culken, John M. "A Schoolman's Guide to Marshall McLuhan." *The Saturday Review*, March 18, 1967, 51–53, 70–72.

Cureton, L. W. "The History of Grading Practices." *National Council on Measurement in Education* 2:4 (May 1971) 1–8.

Csikszentmihalyi, Mihaly. *Flow: The Psychology of Optimal Experience.* New York: Harper & Row, 1990.

Egan, Kieran. *Learning in Depth: A Simple Innovation That Can Transform Schooling.* Chicago: University of Chicago Press, 2010.

Ericsson, Anders, et al. "The Role of Deliberate Practice in the Acquisition of Expert Performance." *Psychological Review* 100:3 (1993) 363–406. http://citeseerx.ist.psu.edu/viewdoc/summary?doi=10.1.1.169.9712.

Foer, Joshua. *Moonwalking with Einstein: The Art and Science of Remembering Everything.* New York: Penguin, 2011.

Frankl, Viktor E. *Man's Search for Meaning.* Boston: Beacon, 2006.

Fuller, R. Buckminster. *Critical Path.* New York: St. Martin's, 1981.

Gatto, John Taylor. *The Underground History of American Education: A Schoolteacher's Intimate Investigation into the Problem of Modern Schooling.* New York: Oxford Village, 2001.

Gardner, Howard, Mihaly Csikszentmihalyi, and William Damon. *Good Work: When Excellence and Ethics Meet.* New York: Basic Books, 2011.

Gilbertson, Annie. "Few LA Students Using Pearson's iPad Software, Survey Shows." Southern California Public Radio (89.3 KPCC). September 18, 2014. http://www.scpr.org/blogs/education/2014/09/18/17312/survey-few-la-students-using-pearson-s-ipad-softwa/.

Gutman, Amy. *Democratic Education.* Princeton, NJ: Princeton University Press, 1999.

Hiss, William, and Valerie Franks. "Defining Promise: Optional Standardized Testing Policies in American Colleges and Universities." February 2014. http://www.nacacnet.org/research/research-data/nacac-research/Documents/DefiningPromise.pdf.

BIBLIOGRAPHY

Holt, Nicholas L. "Representation, Legitimation, and Autoethnography: An Autoethnographic Writing Story." *International Journal of Qualitative Methods* 2:1 (2003). http://www.ualberta.ca/~iiqm/backissues/2_1/html/holt.html.

Hybels, Bill. *Holy Discontent: Fueling the Fire That Ignites Personal Vision.* Grand Rapids: Zondervan, 2007.

Illich, Ivan. *Disabling Professions.* London: M. Boyars, 1977.

James, Michael. "MSNBC: We Have to Break Through This Idea 'That Kids Belong to Their Parents.'" CNSNews, April 8, 2013. http://cnsnews.com/news/article/msnbc-we-have-break-through-idea-kids-belong-their-parents.

Jones, Damon, et al. "Early Social-Emotional Functioning and Public Health: The Relationship between Kindergarten Social Competence and Future Wellness." *American Journal of Public Health* 105:11 (November 2015) 2283–90. http://ajph.aphapublications.org/doi/abs/10.2105/AJPH.2015.302630.

Kamanetz, Anya. "Non-Academic Skills Are Key to Success. But What Should We Call Them?" NPREd, May 28, 2015. http://www.npr.org/sections/ed/2015/05/28/404684712/non-academic-skills-are-key-to-success-but-what-should-we-call-them.

King, Martin Luther, Jr. "The Three Dimensions of a Complete Life." Delivered at New Covenant Baptist Church, Chicago, April 9, 1967. http://kingencyclopedia.stanford.edu/encyclopedia/documentsentry/doc_the_three_dimensions_of_a_complete_life.1.html.

Labaree, David F. *How to Succeed in School without Really Learning: The Credentials Race in American Education.* New Haven, CT: Yale University Press, 1999.

Lopez, Shane J., and Michelle C. Louis. "The Principles of Strengths-Based Education." *Journal of College and Character* 10:4 (April 2009) 1–8. http://www.dowhatmatters.umn.edu/sites/default/files/public/The%20Principles%20of%20Strengths-Based%20Education.pdf.

Mientka, Matthew. "High School GPA 'Strongly Predicts' Future Income, and Later Well-Being." Medical Daily, May 19, 2014. http://www.medicaldaily.com/high-school-gpa-strongly-predicts-future-income-and-later-well-being-283304.

Northwest Evaluation Association. "Measure Student Progress with MAP." https://www.nwea.org/assessments/map/.

Nugent, S. Georgia. "The Tower of Google." Educause 2006 Annual Conference. http://www.educause.edu/annual-conference/2006/2006/tower-google.

Obama, Barack. "President Obama Asks American to Learn Computer Science." December 8, 2013. https://www.youtube.com/watch?v=6XvmhE1J9PY.

———. State of the Union. January 13, 2016. https://www.whitehouse.gov/the-press-office/2016/01/12/remarks-president-barack-obama-%E2%80%93-prepared-delivery-state-union-address.

Oldenburg, Ray. *The Great Good Place: Cafés, Coffee Shops, Community Centers, Beauty Parlors, General Stores, Bars, Hangouts, and How They Get You through the Day.* New York: Paragon House, 1989.

Peterson, Christopher, and Martin E. P. Seligman. *Character Strengths and Virtues: A Handbook and Classification.* Washington, DC: American Psychological Association, 2004.

Postman, Neil. *The End of Education: Redefining the Value of School.* New York: Knopf, 1995.

———. "Five Things We Need to Know about Technological Change." Delivered in Denver, March 28, 1998. http://web.cs.ucdavis.edu/~rogaway/classes/188/materials/postman.pdf.

———. "Informing Ourselves to Death." Delivered to the German Informatics Society (Gesellschaft fuer Informatik) in Stuttgart, October 11, 1990. https://w2.eff.org/Net_culture/Criticisms/informing_ourselves_to_death. paper.

———. "Technology and Society." Delivered at Calvin College, Grand Rapids, January 12, 1998. Video recording online at http://www.c-span.org/video/?98576-1/technology-society and https://www.youtube.com/playlist?list=PL13E676308EB6F00B.

———. *Technopoly: The Surrender of Culture to Technology.* New York: Knopf, 1992.

Rogers, Fred. Interview with Karen Herman for the Archive of American Television. Conducted July 22, 1999. Video recording online at http://www.emmytvlegends.org/interviews/people/fred-rogers.

———. *Life's Journey According to Mr. Rogers.* N.p.: Hyperion Audiobooks, 2005.

Russell, Bertrand. *Why I Am Not a Christian: And Other Essays on Religion and Related Subjects.* New York: Simon and Schuster, 1957.

Sequeira, Sharon. "MLK Quote of the Week: 'All labor that uplifts humanity has dignity and importance and should be undertaken with painstaking excellence.'" The King Center blog, April 9, 2013. http://www.thekingcenter.org/blog/mlk-quote-week-all-labor-uplifts-humanity-has-dignity-and-importance-and-should-be-undertaken.

Sieden, Lloyd Steven. *Buckminster Fuller's Universe: An Appreciation.* New York: Plenum, 1989.

Siemens, George. "Adios EdTech. Hola Something Else." September 9, 2015. http://www.elearnspace.org/blog/2015/09/09/adios-ed-tech-hola-something-else/.

Smith, Peter. *Your Hidden Credentials.* Washington, DC: Acropolis, 1986.

Snyder, Jeffrey Aaron. "Teaching Kids 'Grit' Is All the Rage. Here's What's Wrong with It." *New Republic,* May 6, 2014. https://newrepublic.com/article/117615/problem-grit-kipp-and-character-based-education.

Soave, Robby. "Google Executive: GPA, Test Scores 'Worthless' for Hiring." The Daily Caller, June 20, 2013. http://dailycaller.com/2013/06/20/google-executive-gpa-test-scores-worthless-for-hiring/.

Bibliography

Tough, Paul. *How Children Succeed: Grit, Curiosity, and the Hidden Power of Character*. Boston: Houghton Mifflin Harcourt, 2012.

Turkle, Sherry. *Alone Together: Why We Expect More from Technology and Less from Each Other*. New York: Basic Books, 2011.

Turner, Cory, and Anya Kamentz. "A 'Sizable Decrease' in Those Passing the GED." NPREd, January, 2015. http://www.npr.org/sections/ed/2015/01/09/375440666/a-sizable-decrease-in-those-passing-the-ged.

United Nations General Assembly. "Universal Declaration of Human Rights." Adopted December 10, 1948. http://www.refworld.org/docid/3ae6b3712c.html.

US Department of Education. "Mission." October 20, 2011. http://www2.ed.gov/about/overview/mission/mission.html.

Vidhyashram, Velammal. "No Kidding, This Eighth Grader from Chennai Is Looking to Hire You." *YourStory*, March 28, 2014. http://yourstory.com/2014/03/arjun-lateralogics/.

Williams, Cheryl. "The Science of Good Character . . . Two Schools Journey to Success for Students by Nurturing 'Grit." Learning First Alliance, September 20, 2011. http://www.learningfirst.org/science-good-character.

www.ingramcontent.com/pod-product-compliance
Lightning Source LLC
Chambersburg PA
CBHW070253290326
41930CB00041B/2518